CIVIC CENTER

EBOLA AND MARBURG VIRUSES

Second Edition

DEADLY DISEASES AND EPIDEMICS

Anthrax, Second Edition

Antibiotic-Resistant Bacteria

Avian Flu

Botulism, Second Edition

Campylobacteriosis

Cervical Cancer

Chicken Pox

Cholera, Second Edition

Dengue Fever and Other Hemorrhagic Viruses

Diphtheria

Ebola

Encephalitis

Escherichia coli Infections, Second Edition

Gonorrhea, Second Edition

Hantavirus Pulmonary Syndrome

Helicobacter pylori

Hepatitis

Herpes

HIV/AIDS

Infectious Diseases of the Mouth

Infectious Fungi

Influenza, Second Edition

Legionnaires' Disease

Leprosy

Lung Cancer

Lyme Disease

Mad Cow Disease

Malaria, Second Edition

Meningitis, Second Edition

Mononucleosis, Second Edition

Pelvic Inflammatory Disease

Plague, Second Edition

Polio, Second Edition

Prostate Cancer

Rabies

Rocky Mountain Spotted Fever

Rubella and Rubeola

Salmonella

SARS, Second Edition

Smallpox

Staphylococcus aureus Infections

Streptococcus (Group A), Second Edition

Streptococcus (Group B)

Syphilis, Second Edition

Tetanus

Toxic Shock Syndrome

Trypanosomiasis

Tuberculosis

Tularemia

Typhoid Fever

West Nile Virus, Second Edition

Whooping Cough

Yellow Fever

DEADLY DISEASES AND EPIDEMICS

EBOLA AND MARBURG VIRUSES

Second Edition

Tara C. Smith, Ph.D.

Consulting Editor
Hilary Babcock, M.D., M.P.H.,
Infectious Diseases Division,
Washington University School of Medicine,
Medical Director of Occupational Health (Infectious Diseases),
Barnes-Jewish Hospital and St. Louis Children's Hospital

Foreword by
David L. Heymann
World Health Organization

CHELSEA HOUSE
P U B L I S H E R S
An imprint of Infobase Publishing

Ebola and Marburg Viruses, Second Edition

Chelsea House
An imprint of Infobase Publishing
132 West 31st Street
New York NY 10001

Library of Congress Cataloging-in-Publication Data

Smith, Tara C., 1976–
Ebola and Marburg viruses / Tara C. Smith — 2nd ed.
   p. cm. — (Deadly diseases and epidemics)
Includes bibliographical references and index.
ISBN-13: 978-1-60413-252-6 (hardcover : alk. paper)
ISBN-10: 1-60413-252-3 (hardcover : alk. paper) 1. Ebola virus disease.
2. Marburg virus disease I. Title.
QR201.E16S656 2011
614.5'7—dc22

                    2010032999

Text design by Terry Mallon
Cover design by Takeshi Takahashi
Composition by Mary Susan Ryan-Flynn
Cover printed by Bang Printing, Brainerd, MN
Book printed and bound by Bang Printing, Brainerd, MN
Date printed: November 2010
Printed in the United States of America

10 9 8 7 6 5 4 3 2 1   **3 1232 00893 3147**

Table of Contents

Foreword
David L. Heymann, World Health Organization   6

1. **A Modern Plague**   8

2. **Marburg Virus Emerges**   12

3. **Ebola in Africa and Beyond**   17

4. **General Characteristics of the Viruses**   35

5. **Ecology of the Viruses**   43

6. **Methods of Detection and Treatment**   58

7. **Developing a Vaccine**   66

8. **Other Hemorrhagic Fevers**   75

Notes   85

Glossary   86

Bibliography   92

Further Resources   97

Index   98

Communicable diseases kill and cause long-term disability. The microbial agents that cause them are dynamic, changeable, and resilient: They are responsible for more than 14 million deaths each year, mainly in developing countries.

Approximately 46% of all deaths in the developing world are due to communicable diseases, and almost 90% of these deaths are from AIDS, tuberculosis, malaria, and acute diarrheal and respiratory infections of children. In addition to causing great human suffering, these high-mortality communicable diseases have become major obstacles to economic development. They are a challenge to control either because of the lack of effective vaccines, or because the drugs that are used to treat them are becoming less effective because of antimicrobial drug resistance.

Millions of people, especially those who are poor and living in developing countries, are also at risk from disabling communicable diseases such as polio, leprosy, lymphatic filariasis, and onchocerciasis. In addition to human suffering and permanent disability, these communicable diseases create an economic burden—both on the workforce that handicapped persons are unable to join, and on their families and society, upon which they must often depend for economic support.

Finally, the entire world is at risk of the unexpected communicable diseases, those that are called emerging or re-emerging infections. Infection is often unpredictable because risk factors for transmission are not understood, or because it often results from organisms that cross the species barrier from animals to humans. The cause is often viral, such as Ebola and Marburg hemorrhagic fevers and severe acute respiratory syndrome (SARS). In addition to causing human suffering and death, these infections place health workers at great risk and are costly to economies. Infections such as Bovine Spongiform Encephalopathy (BSE) and the associated new human variant of Creutzfeldt-Jakob disease (vCJD) in Europe, and avian influenza A (H5N1) in Asia, are reminders of the seriousness of emerging and re-emerging infections. In addition, many of these infections have the potential to cause pandemics, which are a constant threat to our economies and public health security.

Science has given us vaccines and anti-infective drugs that have helped keep infectious diseases under control. Nothing demonstrates

6

the effectiveness of vaccines better than the successful eradication of smallpox, the decrease in polio as the eradication program continues, and the decrease in measles when routine immunization programs are supplemented by mass vaccination campaigns.

Likewise, the effectiveness of anti-infective drugs is clearly demonstrated through prolonged life or better health in those infected with viral diseases such as AIDS, parasitic infections such as malaria, and bacterial infections such as tuberculosis and pneumococcal pneumonia.

But current research and development is not filling the pipeline for new anti-infective drugs as rapidly as resistance is developing, nor is vaccine development providing vaccines for some of the most common and lethal communicable diseases. At the same time, providing people with access to existing anti-infective drugs, vaccines, and goods such as condoms or bed nets—necessary for the control of communicable diseases in many developing countries—remains a great challenge.

Education, experimentation, and the discoveries that grow from them are the tools needed to combat high mortality infectious diseases, diseases that cause disability, or emerging and re-emerging infectious diseases. At the same time, partnerships between developing and industrialized countries can overcome many of the challenges of access to goods and technologies. This book may inspire its readers to set out on the path of drug and vaccine development, or on the path to discovering better public health technologies by applying our current understanding of the human genome and those of various infectious agents. Readers may likewise be inspired to help ensure wider access to those protective goods and technologies. Such inspiration, with pragmatic action, will keep us on the winning side of the struggle against communicable diseases.

David L. Heymann
Assistant Director General
Health Security and Environment
Representative of the Director General for Polio Eradication
World Health Organization
Geneva, Switzerland

1

A Modern Plague

In 1967 a mysterious infection hit laboratory workers in Marburg, Germany, and Belgrade, in the former Yugoslavia. Twenty-five workers, busily carrying out research on the polio virus, came down with a similar set of symptoms: fever, diarrhea, vomiting, **shock**, and eventually circulatory system collapse. The fear spread when individuals who had contact with these scientists also became ill. Two doctors and a nurse who took care of the workers came down with the same infection, as did an autopsy attendant and the wife of a veterinarian who worked at the initial facility. Doctors were puzzled. Initially they thought it may have been typhoid fever, a bacterial infection caused by *Salmonella typhi,* due to the nausea and vomiting patients experienced. However, no bacteria could be isolated from the sick workers.

More frighteningly, many of the patients were experiencing severe bleeding. It was difficult for the doctors and nurses treating them to even draw blood, as needle puncture sites simply started to bleed. In all, 31 people were infected and 7 (23%) of them died from the disease.

Tests were being conducted in earnest to find the agent causing the disease, but they came back negative for most of the common infectious suspects. Finally, using a powerful microscope, scientists were able to see what appeared to be a previously undescribed type of virus in the tissues of animals infected with blood from human patients. This new virus was confirmed and named Marburg, after the city where most of the cases had originated. The virus was found to exhibit a morphology (shape) unlike any previously known virus. Because of this, it was placed into a new group, termed the Filoviridae.

While one group of scientists was trying to determine the causative agent, another group was working on an examination of the epidemiology of the outbreak—looking at patterns that were common to the patients in order to determine the origin of the infection. Investigators determined that all of the

8

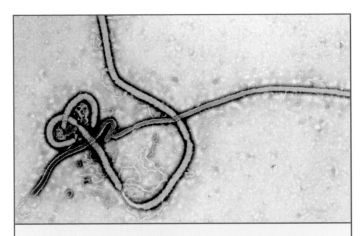

Figure 1.1 Scanning electron micrograph of the Ebola virus. Its thread-like appearance led to its designation as a "filovirus." (Centers for Disease Control and Prevention)

primary cases—those who had gotten ill from the original source, rather than the doctors and nurses who were infected by the ill individuals—all worked in various aspects of polio vaccine development. They also all had direct contact with blood, organs, and cell cultures from *Cercopithecus aethiops* monkeys—"African green monkeys"— which had been imported from Uganda. These monkeys were used mainly for the production of kidney cell cultures, which were used to grow the polio virus in order to produce vaccine.[1]

This outbreak was the world's first introduction to the filovirus family, but far from its last.

A SECOND FILOVIRUS

In 1976, almost a decade after the initial outbreak, both the Democratic Republic of the Congo (formerly Zaire) and Sudan were experiencing devastating outbreaks of a deadly **hemorrhagic** (bleeding) fever. Because travel was difficult in and around the areas of Sudan and the Democratic Republic of the Congo, outsiders were still unaware of the outbreaks weeks after they began. In fact, the epidemics were largely over by the time teams of scientists from the Centers for Disease Control and Prevention (CDC) arrived on the scene. Fortunately, scientists were able to look back and examine the outbreaks by piecing together data from survivors. Scientists determined that the causative agent for these outbreaks was a virus similar to Marburg, another filovirus. This virus was named Ebola, for the Ebola River that crosses the village of Yambuku in the Democratic Republic of the Congo.

Since the 1976 Ebola outbreak, the virus has occasionally resurfaced in human populations. The exact source of these outbreaks and where the virus "hides" between epidemics are unknown. A small outbreak was reported in Sudan in 1979, and one case was reported in the Democratic Republic of the Congo in 1977. The virus did not truly capture the fascination of American scientists, however, until Ebola surfaced within the United States in 1989, in a primate research facility in in Reston, Virginia (just outside Washington, D.C.). The subtype of Ebola virus in this outbreak was different from those that had been isolated in human outbreaks in Africa, and was named Ebola-Reston. No humans died in the Reston outbreak, although the virus was fatal to monkeys.

Ebola has resurfaced in Africa several times since the first outbreaks in the 1970s. These outbreaks will be discussed in later chapters.

WHY ARE FILOVIRUSES SO FASCINATING?

With all the media attention that Marburg and Ebola viruses have received, one may think they have been a major cause of mortality in humans, similar to previous deadly diseases, such as the plague. However, this is a misconception. In over 40 years, Marburg and Ebola have caused fewer than 2,500 known human infections, resulting in approximately 1,800 deaths. When compared to a virus such as influenza, which is responsible for approximately 36,000 deaths in just one typical year in the United States alone, one cannot help but wonder why filoviruses have received reputations as terrible killers. However, total deaths are not the entire picture. With the exception of rabies and AIDS, no known virus kills with the effectiveness of filoviruses. In the following chapters, we will examine the many factors that make filoviruses worthy of study from a scientist's point of view. We will also discuss why viruses that have caused relatively few deaths, almost all of them in Africa, have become so feared around the world.

KNOWN OUTBREAKS OF FILOVIRAL DISEASE

1967: Germany, Marburg virus discovered, 31 cases (23% mortality rate)

1975: Marburg in Zimbabwe and South Africa, 3 cases, 1 death (33% mortality)

1976–1977: Concurrent outbreaks in DRC/Zaire (319 cases, 90% mortality) and Sudan (284 cases, 53% mortality)

1979: Ebola outbreak in the Sudan: 34 cases (65% mortality)

1980: Marburg in Kenya, 2 cases (50% mortality)

1987: Marburg in Kenya, 1 case (100% mortality)

1989: U.S.S.R., 2 laboratory accidents (50% mortality)

1994: Ebola in Ivory Coasty, 1 case (100% mortality); Gabon, 51 cases (61% mortality)

1995: DRC Ebola outbreak, 315 cases (81% mortality)

1996: Two Ebola outbreaks in Gabon, 91 total cases (73% mortality); South Africa, 1 case (76% mortality)

1998–2000: Marburg in DRC, 150 cases (mortality ranging from 56%–82%)

2000: Ebola in Uganda, at least 425 cases (53% mortality)

2001–2002: Ebola in Gabon, 65 cases (82% mortality); Republic of Congo, 58 cases (76% mortality)

2002–2003: Republic of Congo, 143 cases (89% mortality)

2003: Republic of Congo, 35 cases (83% mortality)

2004: Sudan, 17 cases (41% mortality)

2007: Democratic Republic of Congo, 264 cases (71% mortality)

2007–2008: Uganda, 149 cases (25% mortality)

2008: Philippines, 6 cases (0% mortality)

2008–2009: Democratic Republic of Congo, 32 cases (47% mortality)

2
Marburg Virus Emerges

Though Marburg was the first filovirus discovered (in 1967), only 7 additional human infections with this virus were seen in the next 30 years, a number far outpaced by Ebola infections. More recently, as large outbreaks in Africa due to Marburg virus have been recognized. One began in 1998 in the Democratic Republic of Congo, and lasted until 2000. The second was recognized in Angola in early 2005, and had killed 117 people (94% mortality rate) as of April of that year.

In the original outbreak in Marburg, Germany (caused by imported African monkeys), a total of 31 cases (7 deaths) resulted. After this episode, the virus went back into hiding for almost a decade, not surfacing again until 1975, in South Africa. The origin of this outbreak is unknown, although based on epidemiological studies it is assumed that the **index case** (the first person known to have been infected), a young man hitchhiking through Africa, acquired the disease in Zimbabwe, and then infected two other people in South Africa when he arrived there. Only the index case died from the disease; the **secondary cases** (those infected due to contact with the index case) survived.

Marburg again disappeared until a case was reported in Kenya in 1980, and another in 1987, in the same area. In the first outbreak, again only the index case died, while a second patient survived. Only one infection was noted in the 1987 outbreak, resulting in the death of the patient. Both of these Kenyan outbreaks occurred in the vicinity of Mount Elgon, and there is evidence that both index cases had spent time in a cave inside the mountain. This has led to unconfirmed speculation that bats may be a **reservoir** for filoviruses.

Between 1987 and 1998, the only cases of Marburg were due to laboratory accidents, both in the former Soviet Union. One of these cases was fatal. However, in 1998, the largest natural outbreak of Marburg virus disease began in northeastern Democratic Republic of the Congo (DRC). This time, the focus of the outbreak was a town called Durba (population 16,000). A large number of men in this region worked for the Kilo Moto Mining Company, which ran a number of illegal gold mines in the area. Working conditions in this area were precarious. Civil war broke out in 1996, and the socioeconomic situation deteriorated ever further. Infectious diseases of all types were common, as vaccinations and medication were in short supply. The Marburg outbreak is thought to have started in November 1998, although it was not reported to any international agencies until late April 1999, following the death of the chief medical officer in the area.

At that time, local officials contacted *Medecins sans Frontieres* (Doctors without Borders) in Belgium regarding the ongoing epidemic. Officers were sent to investigate and to curb the spread of the epidemic. Scientists immediately sent patient samples to the National Institute of Virology in Johannesburg, South Africa. The lab diagnosed Marburg virus as the cause of the illness on May 6. **Barrier nursing procedures** were instituted, and isolation wards were instituted at the hospital. From June 1999 until December 2000, 30 confirmed and 45 suspected cases of Marburg were identified. The mortality rate was 56% for confirmed cases of Marburg. In contrast, the same number of cases was identified retrospectively between November 1998 and May 1999, with 62 deaths (82% mortality rate). Miners were found to be at a significantly higher risk of contracting Marburg than the general population of this area, suggesting they may be more frequently exposed to the natural reservoir of Marburg virus.

A new larger outbreak of Marburg was reported in the southwestern African country of Angola in the spring of 2005. Studies showed the outbreak had actually started in

November 2004 but was not brought to the attention of international authorities until March 2005. A reason for this delay was the lack of medical personnel and facilities in the area:

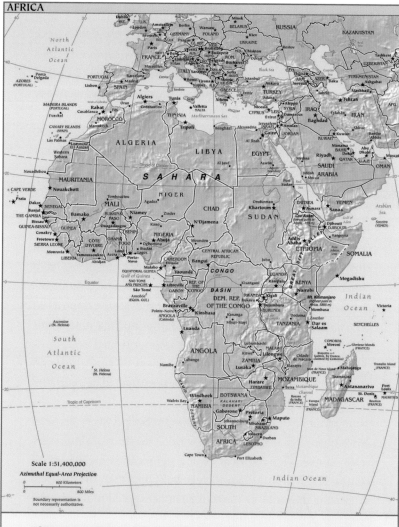

Figure 2.1 Map of Africa. Ebola cases have been found in Sudan, Uganda, Gabon, Democratic Republic of the Congo (DRC), Cote d'Ivoire (Ivory Coast), while Marburg cases have occurred in Zimbabwe, South Africa, Kenya, DRC, and Angola. (CIA Maps and Publications)

the province in which the outbreak took place had only one hospital and four doctors to serve a population of 1.5 million people. The last case in the area was diagnosed in late July, and the outbreak was declared officially over in November 2005.

This outbreak was not only the largest, it is also one of the deadliest infectious disease outbreaks known. Of 252 confirmed infections, 227 deaths were recorded—approximately a 90% mortality rate. Many of the deaths were among children and health care workers, who were exposed to high concentrations of the virus due to participation in funeral rituals or patient care.

Marburg reappeared in 2007 in Uganda, beginning in individuals employed in gold mining. The first identified case was a 29-year-old man who contracted the infection in early July and was admitted to the hospital a few days later. He died on July 14, 2007. An investigation showed that he had had close contact with a co-worker, who had suffered a similar illness (but recovered) a few weeks prior. Though other individuals who had close contact with these individuals were examined, no other cases were confirmed.

Marburg reappeared one more time in Europe in 2008. A 40-year-old woman from the Netherlands had traveled to Uganda for a three-week vacation in May 2008. On June 19, she visited two caves in the Maramagambo forest, which were known to be populated with fruit bats. A few days after she returned home, she became ill, and was admitted to a Dutch hospital on July 5, where she later died. No other cases were identified.

It appears that Marburg is probably **endemic** (always present) in some areas in Africa, particularly Uganda and the DRC. Thus, sporadic cases of the disease are to be expected. Instability and conflict in this region make it difficult to supply regular international aid, making future outbreaks in these areas likely. More information on the reservoir and transmission of this virus would go a long way toward controlling filovirus infections in Africa. New research examining these factors will be discussed in Chapter 5.[1]

MARBURG VIRUS RISK FACTORS

In addition to the outbreaks of Marburg virus infection, a number of studies have also examined serological evidence of prior infection with Marburg virus. These studies look in the blood of participants for **antibodies** to Marburg, which are proteins that act as markers of a past infection. One such study was carried out following the 1998–1999 outbreak in Durba in the Democratic Republic of Congo. Many of the individuals in this area are involved in gold mining; farming and hunting are also common. Individuals in the area were aware of frequent Marburg-like illnesses; the villagers dubbed these "Durba hemorrhagic syndrome" or "Durba syndrome" and associated it with working in the mines.

Study participants were asked about a number of factors that might put one at higher risk of exposure to Marburg virus, including activity in the mines, exposure to people with Durba syndrome or having suffered from Durba syndrome themselves, and exposure to a number of different animal species who may carry the virus (including rodents, bats, and monkeys).

Antibodies to Marburg were found in 2% of this population (15 out of 912 participants). Thirteen of those were miners; the other two were housewives who had both reported caring for a family member who had Durba syndrome, having contact with their body fluids, and participating in their burial, which may have been how they were exposed to Marburg virus. The study showed that miners were approximately 14 times more likely to have Marburg antibodies than those who were not miners, suggesting that these mines and caves are a site for infection with the Marburg virus and exposure to the animal or insect reservoir that carries the virus.[2]

3

Ebola in Africa and Beyond

1976—EBOLA FIRST APPEARS IN AFRICA

It had been nearly a decade since the deadly Marburg virus had been discovered in Germany. In the interim, epidemics of hemorrhagic fever came and went in Africa, fueled by viruses such as those that cause Lassa and yellow fever. In 1976, however, an epidemic of grand proportion was erupting in Zaire [now Democratic Republic of the Congo (DRC)]. It was an epidemic unlike any caused by the Lassa or yellow fever viruses.

The Ebola outbreak likely began in August 1976, when a patient named Mabalo visited the Yambuku Mission Hospital in Yambuku, Zaire, seeking treatment for a high fever. He had recently returned from a mission trip around northern Zaire, and he assumed he had contracted malaria. One of the "nurses" on staff (actually a Belgian nun with no formal medical training) administered an injection of quinine, a drug used to treat malaria. The patient returned home to rest. The hospital was short on supplies, so the needle used to inject Mabalo was reused on other hospital patients.

Despite the hospital's best efforts, Mabalo succumbed to his illness and died on September 8, 1976. He was the index case. In accordance with regional tradition, Mabalo's body was ritually prepared for burial by his wife, mother, and other female friends and relatives. All food and waste was removed from the body, a procedure often performed using bare hands. Within weeks of Mabalo's death, 21 of his friends and family members, many of whom had been involved in preparing his body for burial, contracted the infection that had killed him. Eighteen of them died from the disease.

The hospital staff members quickly realized that they were dealing with a disease unlike anything they had ever seen. Shortly after Mabalo's death, the hospital was crowded with people showing signs of this disease. Patients were bleeding from the gums, eyes, and rectum. Panic had invaded the area, and people were beginning to flee to more remote locations, possibly carrying the disease with them. Even the staff at the hospital was beginning to exhibit signs of the disease.

Meanwhile, samples from patients who had died as a result of the disease made their way to the World Health Organization (WHO) in Geneva, Switzerland, and the Centers for Disease Control and Prevention (CDC) in Atlanta, Georgia. Scientists studying the samples recognized their similarity to the Marburg virus. They also recognized that a similar outbreak was occurring to the north in Sudan.

The death toll and the extent of infection were incredible. Forty-six villages around Yambuku were affected. The final tally showed 358 cases and 325 deaths, a fatality rate of 90.7%—higher than almost any known infectious agent. In this epidemic, as would be the case in several later outbreaks, **nosocomial** (hospital-based) spread was a critical factor in the early spread of the disease. The clinic in Yambuku was impoverished, and supplies were limited. Only five syringes were issued to its nurses each morning, and they were used and reused on between 300 and 600 patients each day. Later studies have shown that only a few viral particles are needed to cause an active infection. Dirty needles were an incredibly efficient way to transmit the virus from one patient to another. Had the epidemic within the hospital not spread so virulently, perhaps the ramifications would have been less severe.

SIMILAR HORROR IN SUDAN
Once these epidemics were recognized by the world community, both the WHO and the CDC sent scientists to investigate and assist in ending the outbreak. One of these investigators,

Dr. Joe McCormick, traveled from Yambuku to Sudan in order to assess the extent of the epidemic there. His trip was dangerous and difficult. He traveled on terrible "roads," which were often more like poorly maintained dirt paths. At the Sudanese border, he encountered an Italian Catholic mission. Dr. McCormick was informed by the priests working there that an epidemic was under way around the Sudanese village of N'zara, 400 miles from Yambuku. Dr. McCormick investigated for three weeks in and around N'zara, interviewing patients and family members of the dead, and collecting blood samples. As had been done in Yambuku, barrier nursing procedures were instituted, and the epidemic slowly subsided. The final result showed that 284 people had been infected and 151 died from the disease, resulting in a 53% fatality rate, lower than that of the Yambuku outbreak.

N'zara, at the time, was a city of about 20,000 people, with a cotton factory at the center of its economy. Some 2,000 men worked in this facility, under poor conditions. Large numbers of bats congregated in the roofing inside the building. Later investigations showed that on June 27, a man who worked at the factory fell ill. He died on July 6 of **hemorrhage** (massive bleeding). His death was followed by the deaths of two coworkers, both of whom worked in same room as the primary case. By September, at least 35 deaths had occurred among employees of the cotton factory and their families. Similar to the Yambuku outbreak, this one also multiplied in the hospital at N'zara due to poor medical practices. The virus spread to more than one-third of the hospital staff and killed 41 people. Many people fled as the epidemic raced through the facility.

Still unanswered at this point was the question of whether these two outbreaks were unrelated, or whether they had been triggered by a common source. The question was definitively answered in the early 1990s by sequencing the actual viruses that had been isolated during these epidemics and finding that they were different strains. In 1976, however, the technology needed to do this did not yet exist. Dr. McCormick argued that the two outbreaks were separate. He reasoned that there were no common roads. In fact, the ones that connected the two villages were practically impassible. In addition, no villages between the two outbreak sites had been affected, as one would expect if the source of the outbreak had come from a third site and spread to both Yambuku and N'zara. Finally, the strains appeared to differ somewhat in **virulence**. The virus that was responsible for the N'zara outbreak seemed to spread more easily than the one in Yambuku, but it caused death less often. It turned out that Dr. McCormick was correct. The Ebola Zaire strain caused the 1976 Yambuku epidemic, while the Ebola Sudan strain caused the outbreak in N'zara.

A smaller, but still significant, Ebola outbreak occurred again near N'zara in Sudan. On August 2, 1979, a man with fever, diarrhea, and vomiting was admitted to the hospital in N'zara. He died three days later. The hospital had not practiced isolation measures or barrier nursing procedures. By late August, the illness had spread throughout the community and the hospital, leading to 34 infections and 22 deaths (a 65% mortality rate). Again, the source of the epidemic appeared to be the cotton factory.

EBOLA PLAYS HIDE AND SEEK
Following the 1979 outbreak in Sudan, Ebola went into hiding in Africa. **Epidemiologists** frantically traced leads, trying to find its hiding place, but they were not successful. Though a less deadly strain emerged in the United States, Ebola disappeared in Africa for 15 years, before it returned with a vengeance.

The first sign that the deadly virus had returned occurred on Africa's Ivory Coast. It was the first time the virus had surfaced in West Africa. In November 1994, a researcher was investigating an epidemic among chimpanzees in the Taï National Forest. The epidemic had killed half the population of chimpanzees in a two-year period. The scientist, who had recently performed a **necropsy** on a wild chimpanzee, fell ill with high fever, headache, chills, abdominal pain, diarrhea, and vomiting. Thinking she had contracted malaria, the scientist was treated with halofantrine, an anti-malarial drug. Her symptoms continued to get worse, and she was flown back to her native Switzerland on the seventh day of her illness. She was treated in a hospital isolation room. She was not tested for any form of hemorrhagic fever, as she had no obvious bleeding, and Ebola had not yet been found in Switzerland.

In December of that year, scientists began an epidemiologic investigation to discover the cause of the chimpanzee's death. The investigation helped to isolate a new subtype of Ebola—Ebola Côte d'Ivoire. Scientists then examined the researcher for the presence of antibodies to the Ebola virus, and she was found to be positive. This meant that she had been previously infected with the Ebola virus, even though it had not been diagnosed at the time. She recovered from her illness, and there were no secondary cases. Ebola was back, however, and it was not only on the Ivory Coast.

That same year, over 1,000 miles to the southeast in Gabon, another outbreak occurred, and it seemed to be connected to gold mining camps. There were actually two waves of the epidemic. The first outbreak began in December 1994, with a second wave of patients in January and February 1995. A total of 44 people were infected, and 57% of them died. The political situation in Gabon at the time was unstable due to a contentious election rife with irregularities; this made it difficult for researchers to collect data properly, but they did receive reports of a similar epidemic occurring in great apes (chimpanzees and gorillas) in the region. One patient reported that he had recently killed a chimpanzee exhibiting abnormal behavior. Though the epidemic appeared to have started in the mining camps, it was also spread via traditional healers. These healers advocate frequent touching and holding of the victims, and in some cases, even cut the patients' skin with unsterile knives.

Additionally, they advocate traditional burial practices, which include more contact with the corpse and often a ritual washing. These practices serve to increase the risk of contracting the Ebola virus due to virus either on the skin or in the blood or other body secretions. The epidemic was declared over by Gabonese health authorities in mid-February 1995, after no new cases had been reported for several weeks.

In the spring of 1996, another outbreak occurred in a separate village in Gabon, approximately 25 miles south of the original outbreak site. Eighteen patients became ill after butchering and eating a dead chimpanzee they had found. It is not known if they acquired the virus by eating the contaminated meat, accidental cuts during the butchering process, or direct exposure to the skin. Six additional secondary cases and **tertiary cases** (infection due to contact with the secondary cases) were identified. There were six total deaths.

A third outbreak occurred in the fall of that same year, again following a reported chimpanzee epidemic in the area. This time, the victims were all associated with a logging camp. This epidemic lasted through March 1997, resulting in a total of 60 cases and 45 deaths. Sequencing of the glycoprotein gene of this virus revealed that each of these outbreaks was due to an independent introduction of the virus into the human population. In other words, each epidemic was considered separate, even though they all occurred within a relatively short period.

As scientists and doctors were processing the information from the Ivory Coast infection and trying to stem outbreaks in Gabon, a raging epidemic of the disease broke out in Kikwit, in the Democratic Republic of the Congo. By the time investigators were notified of the outbreak in May 1995, the epidemic was already at least two months old. The outbreak was traced back to a charcoal worker who died of hemorrhagic fever in January 1995 at the Kikwit General Hospital. At least three members of his family died as well. From January to March, an additional ten fatal cases occurred in members of his extended family. From there, the epidemic spread to other individuals in adjacent villages and within the hospital setting. As had been the case with the 1976 Ebola outbreak in the Democratic Republic of the Congo, nosocomial transmission played a role in the epidemic. Several patients were believed to have contracted the disease via direct contact with infected patients during surgery or other medical procedures. Deaths included members of the hospital staff. A total of 315 cases of Ebola hemorrhagic fever were identified based on **serological evidence**, viral isolation, and retrospective case analysis. There were 244 deaths, resulting in a 78% mortality rate. The last identified patient died on July 16, 1995, and the epidemic was declared over shortly after that. Subsequent studies have shown that both the Gabon outbreaks and the Kikwit outbreak in the Democratic Republic of the Congo were due to the deadly Zaire strain of Ebola.

Ebola struck yet again, in August 2000, this time in Uganda, in east central Africa (Uganda borders both Sudan and DRC; Figure 3.1). The first patient died in Gulu on September 17, 2000. Despite an investigation, doctors were unable to determine where or how she had contracted the disease. Her death was followed by the deaths of her husband, two children, and several other family members. Authorities reported this information to the Ministry of Health in October of that year, near the peak of the epidemic. An investigation and intervention to control the disease followed, and officials declared the epidemic to be over in January 2001 (Figure 3.2). A total of 425 patients from three villages (Gulu, Masindi, and Mbarara) across Uganda were identified based on symptoms and/or laboratory data. In an eerie echo of the 1976 Ebola outbreak in Sudan, 224 patients died, with a resulting mortality rate of 53%. Indeed, sequence analysis showed the infecting strain to be the Sudan subtype of Ebola. This was the first time this type had surfaced since the 1979 outbreak in Sudan. Scientists hypothesized that Sudanese rebels who carried out regular attacks around Gulu may have accidentally introduced the virus in some manner, though this has never been confirmed.

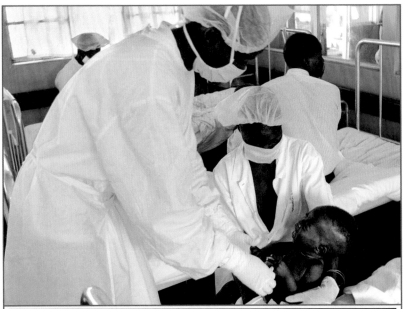

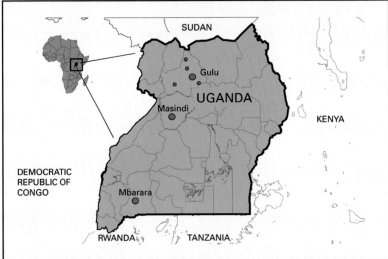

* Persons initially identified by the mobile teams or assessed by a health-care worker (suspect and probable cases using the notification scheme) who were not laboratory negative and met the following case definition: a) unexplained bleeding; or b) fever and three or more specified symptoms (i.e., headache, vomiting, anorexia, diarrhea, weakness or severe fatigue, abdominal pains, body aches or joint pains, difficulty in swallowing, difficulty in breathing, and hiccups); or c) unexplained deaths. All laboratory-confirmed cases also were included.

Figure 3.1 Top: A health care worker examines a patient suspected of Ebola infection in a hospital near Gulu, Uganda, during the October 2000 Ebola outbreak. Bottom: At least three villages in Uganda were infected by the 2000–2001 Ebola Sudan outbreak. (© AP Images/Centers for Disease Control and Prevention)

In the early part of the twenty-first century, the recognition of Ebola outbreaks accelerated. An outbreak straddling the border between the Republic of Congo and Gabon occurred in 2001–2002. The Republic of Congo shares a border with the Democratic Republic of Congo; so while this was the first report of Ebola in the Republic of Congo, filoviruses had been found previously in nearby countries (Ebola previously in the DRC and Gabon, and Marburg in Angola). This outbreak was caused by the Zaire strain of Ebola, and caused 57 illnesses and 43 deaths (75% mortality). The outbreak appears to have begun in a single family, which experienced 5 deaths from Ebola over a three-week period in October 2001. International authorities began investigating in November, and confirmed the Ebola infections. The outbreak was difficult to control due to the remoteness of the villages, and because of ongoing conflict in the affected areas. Interestingly, both villagers and wildlife biologists noticed wildlife deaths (mostly nonhuman primates, including chimpanzees and gorillas) at the same time as the human outbreak.

The Republic of Congo suffered additional outbreaks of Ebola Zaire at the end of 2002, beginning again in December and lasting through March 2003. The index cases for this outbreak, which sickened 143 and killed 128 (89% mortality), were found to be hunters who had recently killed a variety of animals, including antelope and gorilla. Ebola returned to the country again in November 2003, but this outbreak was smaller and shorter-lived than the previous two. Thirty-five individuals were infected, of whom 29 died (83% mortality); the outbreak was contained and over by December 2003. Another small outbreak occurred in April and May 2005, infecting 12 and killing 9 (75% mortality) according to World Health Organization Surveillance data from that year.

Ebola reappeared in Sudan in May 2004 when 7 patients were diagnosed with the disease over a 3-week period. Once again, the index case in this outbreak was reported to have butchered and eaten a baboon in the days prior to onset of disease; it is suspected that this was how he was exposed to

Ebola. In this outbreak, the Sudan strain was responsible, causing 17 illnesses and 7 deaths (41% mortality). The outbreak was quickly contained and officially declared over in June 2004.

It appeared that Ebola was returning to its old haunts in 2007, when the Democratic Republic of Congo was again hit with an outbreak of Ebola Zaire between September and November. Though the outbreak was brief, it was deadly: 264 were infected and 187 were killed (71% mortality). The index cases were traced back to the burial of village chieftains, which could have been infected and spread the infection via burial rites. Ebola returned to this area again in 2008, infecting 21 and killing at least 9 (43% mortality). This caused Angola to temporarily shut down its border with the Democratic Republic of Congo in order to contain the disease.

Ebola returned to Uganda in August 2007, causing 149 illnesses and 37 deaths until the outbreak was declared over in February 2008. This mortality (36%) was significantly lower than most Ebola outbreaks. Interestingly, when scientists tested this virus, it also reacted strangely with their assays. Therefore, they determined the entire molecular sequence of the virus, and found that it was a whole new strain of Ebola, which they named Ebola Bundibugyo.

Finally, Ebola Reston reappeared for the first time in 12 years in the Philippines. However, unlike previous outbreaks of Ebola Reston, which were recognized in non-human primate species, this virus was first found in tests of pigs from several different farms. The pigs had been sick, and samples from dead pigs were sent to the United States in order to determine what was causing the illness. It is thought that the pigs probably acquired the infection from infected bats. Six exposed humans were also found to be positive for antibodies to Ebola Reston, including swine farmers and a butcher, showing that the virus could be transferred from pigs to humans (though none of them reported getting sick, similar to previous Ebola Reston outbreaks transmitted to human from animals).

Though we have learned much about Ebola over the past 30 years, the findings of new strains of the virus and new susceptible

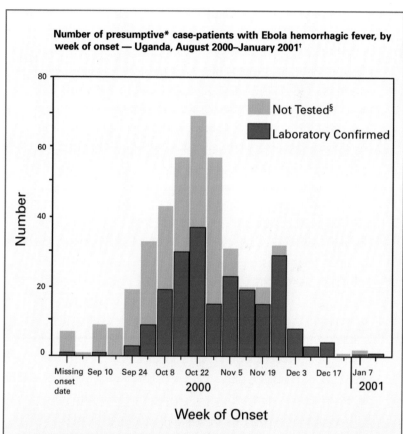

Number of presumptive* case-patients with Ebola hemorrhagic fever, by week of onset — Uganda, August 2000–January 2001[†]

Not Tested[§]

Laboratory Confirmed

Week of Onset

* Persons initially identified by the mobile teams or assessed by a health-care worker (suspect and probable cases using the notification scheme) who were not laboratory negative and met the following case definition: a) unexplained bleeding; or b) fever and three or more specified symptoms (i.e., headache, vomiting, anorexia, diarrhea, weakness or severe fatigue, abdominal pains, body aches or joint pains, difficulty in swallowing, difficulty in breathing, and hiccups); or c) unexplained deaths. All laboratory-confirmed cases were also included.

[†] n=425.

[§] Persons meeting presumptive definition but no specimens collected or laboratory tested.

Figure 3.2 Epidemic curve of the 2000–2001 Ebola outbreak in Uganda. The epidemic peaked in mid-October and was declared over at the end of January 2001, with a total of 224 cases. (Centers for Disease Control and Prevention)

animal species show us just how far we have to go in order to really understand this organism.[1]

EBOLA HITS CLOSE TO HOME

In the fall of 1989, a shipment of 100 wild monkeys from the Philippines arrived at Hazelton Research Products in Reston, Virginia. The particular species was a type of macaque, commonly known as "crab-eater monkeys" (Figure 3.3). Scientists divided the monkeys among 12 different rooms (designated A through L). Workers at the facility noticed that two of the monkeys were dead on arrival. At the time, this was not perceived as an unusual event, as animals occasionally die during transport. The whole world would shortly learn, however, just how unusual these deaths were.

By November 1, 1989, a total of 29 monkeys had died. Most of these deaths had occurred in room F. A necropsy of two monkeys showed the presence of an enlarged spleen, and blood in their intestines. Scientists initially suspected a virus called **simian hemorrhagic fever**. The virus causes a bleeding disease in monkeys (similar to Ebola), but it is not harmful to humans. The microbiologists at Hazelton decided to call in important officials to test their virus. They enlisted the help of virologists at **USAMRIID** (U.S. Army Medical Research Institute of Infectious Diseases) located at Fort Detrick, Maryland. Scientists there had access to facilities that could contain potentially deadly pathogens. By the end of November, scientists had used a number of different tests and had come to a conclusion about the diagnosis of the disease from which the monkeys were suffering. It was Ebola. The new strain was named Ebola Reston, after the place where it was first isolated.

In early December 1989, all monkeys at Hazelton Research Products were **euthanized** (killed), and the facility was temporarily evacuated to be cleaned and decontaminated. Amazingly, no humans became ill. A second wave of Ebola swept through the facility in January and February 1990 following the importation of a new group of monkeys from the Philippines. Again, no humans were infected, even though one technician had cut

Figure 3.3 Macaques, a type of monkey found in Asia and northern Africa, are commonly used in biomedical research in the United States. (© AP Images)

himself with a bloody scalpel. Later tests confirmed, however, that at least four people eventually tested positive for exposure to the Ebola Reston virus. They produced antibodies to the virus, which meant that the virus had entered their bodies and multiplied there, but they never developed symptoms of the disease.

BSL LABS

All pathogens that a researcher may work with in the laboratory are divided into four groups, based on their potential hazard to humans. These groups are termed "biological safety levels," or BSL for short. As safety levels increase, so do the precautions needed in the laboratory.

- A BSL-1 laboratory can work on pathogens that have been shown not to be harmful to humans. No special precautions are needed, though gloves and a lab coat are recommended.

- BSL-2 laboratories are used for pathogens that might pose a risk to humans. Many procedures in these labs need to be performed within a biological containment hood, in order to minimize aerosols (mixtures of liquid and gas) that might be generated when using certain procedures (for example, mixing samples). Gloves, lab coats, and other protective equipment (such as goggles or occasionally masks) must be worn. Any infectious waste generated must be sterilized prior to disposal.

- BSL-3 laboratories are used for pathogens that might cause serious illness or even death when a researcher is exposed via inhalation. This means that air flow must take a certain route within the lab. The lab is engineered so that air

One of these people was the technician who cut himself. Exactly how the other people were infected is not clear. They had no history of being pricked by needles or other similar exposures. Scientists assumed the virus spread through the air, entering the lungs of the humans who were exposed, and also spread in this manner between the rooms containing the monkeys. **Electron microscopy** confirmed the presence of Ebola Reston in the air spaces inside the lungs of infected monkeys. This provided always flows from areas of low contamination to areas of higher contamination. Therefore, any infectious agents will not contaminate areas that do not already contain microbes. Respirators may be worn during some procedures.

• BSL-4 laboratories are for pathogens that, like BSL-3 agents, may be transmitted by aerosol. Additionally, BSL-4 agents pose a high risk of life-threatening disease, and for diseases for which there is no vaccine or cure. BSL-4 is the highest containment possible. Researchers work in "space suits" with respirators and the laboratory is under negative air pressure: This means that air is actually flowing into the lab, being sucked in like a low-power vacuum, which prevents the accidental "escape" of any pathogens. Air that leaves the laboratory exits through HEPA filters, which have pores that are too small for any pathogen to pass through. Researchers must be decontaminated before entering and leaving the laboratory. Because of the expense of running these labs, and the dangerous pathogens investigated within, only five such facilities currently exist in the United States, though others are expected to be built in the coming years.

more evidence that the virus was airborne. The Army decided against testing this hypothesis directly, however, for fear that others would mistakenly see it as an attempt to produce airborne Ebola—a possible biological weapon.

This outbreak (and a subsequent outbreak of Ebola Reston among monkeys imported from the Philippines to Italy in 1992) led officials in the United States to modify the procedures used for the transport and quarantine of nonhuman primates

Figure 3.4 Workers in biosafety level (BSL-4) laboratory must carry out their work dressed in "space suits," and undergo extensive decontamination prior to returning to pathogen-free areas. Those who work in these labs do research on the most deadly agents known to mankind. (Centers for Disease Control and Prevention)

USAMRIID

USAMRIID stands for the U.S. Army Medical Research Institute of Infectious Diseases. Located at Fort Detrick, Maryland, USAMRIID conducts research on biological threats, particularly those aimed at the military. USAMRIID has many facilities that are unavailable at most research institutions, including large BSL-3 and BSL-4 laboratories. USAMRIID was instrumental in diagnosing and containing the 1990 Ebola Reston outbreak, and developed a diagnostic assay for that virus, which is now used to screen primates for infection. USAMRIID scientists have worked with the World Health Organization and the Centers for Disease Control and Prevention in various field studies, including that undertaken during and after the 1995 outbreak of Ebola in the Democratic Republic of the Congo. USAMRIID scientists spend a good deal of time working to understand how pathogens cause disease, and looking for vaccine candidates to prevent disease, as well as drugs that may be able to treat disease.

(monkeys and great apes; humans are also a member of the order Primata, and as such, are also classified as primates). In 1994, the Philippines banned the export of wild-caught monkeys to reduce the possibility of transporting Ebola Reston–positive animals. Even these new regulations combined, however, did not completely eliminate the possibility of Ebola Reston resurfacing in primate shipments to the United States.

In 1996, another shipment of monkeys entered the United States (this time at a facility in Texas) from the Philippines. One monkey died while in quarantine after arrival in Texas. The animal later tested positive for antibodies to the Ebola virus. The virus was also isolated from another monkey in the same shipment. Fifty of the 100 monkeys in the group were euthanized. No employees were found to have been exposed to

EBOLA AND THE MEDIA

The early 1990s marked the height of "Ebola mania" in the United States. Even though the virus had been isolated some 15 years earlier and had already broken out several times in Africa, officials in the United States really had not paid much attention to this new disease. AIDS was on everyone's minds, and a minor killer in Africa, even one as horrendous as Ebola, simply did not seem that important. The identification of Ebola Reston in Virginia changed that. Richard Preston's best-selling book, *The Hot Zone*, describing the Reston outbreak, was released in 1994. Laurie Garrett's *The Coming Plague*, which also discussed Ebola virus, came out that same year. The movie *Outbreak*, starring Dustin Hoffman, about an epidemic of an Ebola-like disease in the United States, was released in 1995. Ebola resurfaced in a large outbreak in Kikwit, Democratic Republic of the Congo, in 1995 as well. All these events served to put Ebola in the national spotlight, and Ebola has become synonymous with the term *dread disease*. Although control of the virus within facilities is possible, studies examining the ecology of the virus in the wild have been inconclusive.

the virus, and the quarantine procedures worked well in curtailing the outbreak. Researchers in the Philippines confirmed that a large percentage of monkey deaths in the Philippines were due to infection with the Ebola virus. The Filipino facility from which the monkeys had originated was closed by the Philippine government in 1997.

4

General Characteristics of the Viruses

Filoviruses are **RNA viruses.** Their genetic material—the material that makes up their **genes**—is composed of ribonucleic acid. Their **genomes** (the entire amount of RNA) are fairly small. Each only contains approximately 19,000 base pairs (in comparison, the human genome contains approximately 3 billion base pairs), which encode a mere 7 proteins. Structurally the viruses resemble a length of thread (see Figure 1.1). The viruses generally appear in a long, filamentous form, but they can also be U-shaped, in the shape of a "6" (the "shepherd's crook" appearance), or even circular. Sequence analysis shows the viruses to be most closely related to the paramyxoviruses, which include the viruses that cause such common diseases as measles and mumps.

As mentioned earlier, the filovirus family consists of four distinct subtypes of Ebola virus, and its cousin virus, Marburg. Within each Ebola **subtype,** the viruses are closely related, but there is variability. For example, viruses of the Ebola Zaire type isolated from the 1976 outbreak in Yambuku and the 1995 epidemic in Kikwit, differed in their nucleotide sequence by only approximately 1.6%. Viruses of different subtypes, however, may differ by as much as 40%. Of the Ebola viruses sequenced, the Reston subtype and the Zaire subtype are the most divergent in sequence. Scientists therefore presume that these subtypes are the most distantly related.

CLINICAL SYMPTOMS OF FILOVIRUS INFECTION

The **incubation period** (the time between exposure to the virus and the development of disease) of Ebola virus is 2 to 21 days, and for Marburg virus is 5 to 10 days. This period may vary, depending on the route of exposure and the amount of virus a patient has come in contact with. For instance, a patient injected with a large amount of filoviruses due to reuse of a dirty needle may develop symptoms more quickly than someone exposed via external contact with a small amount of other bodily fluids from an infected patient. Symptoms, including fever, chills, headache, muscle and joint aches, tiredness, and a general ill feeling, typically appear suddenly. Because these symptoms are common to many diseases, it is very difficult to make a definitive diagnosis of filovirus infection at this stage. As the disease proceeds, bloody diarrhea, a severe sore throat, and **jaundice** (a yellowing of the skin and eyes, due to a buildup of a liver protein) are common symptoms. Vomiting and **anorexia** (loss of appetite) are often seen. Around the fifth day of illness, a short-lived rash may be present. If the patient lives long enough, the rash will often peel, in a manner similar to a severe sunburn.

PATHOGENESIS OF FILOVIRUS INFECTION

The most prominent components of filovirus infection are hemorrhage and **disseminated intravascular coagulation (DIC)**, which means that the blood is actually clotting throughout the body within the capillaries. This process can quickly exhaust the body's supply of the proteins involved in clotting, making the blood unable to respond correctly when actual tissue damage occurs. Uncontrolled bleeding can result.

When filoviruses infect different types of cells, they cause the release of a number of chemicals, including molecules called **cytokines, chemokines**, and **histamines**. Releasing these proteins into the bloodstream causes a number of symptoms of filoviruses infection, including fever, swelling, and shock (a dangerous drop in blood pressure). Shock is a result of these proteins increasing the permeability of the endothelial cells that line the blood vessels. This allows water to leak from the blood into the surrounding tissues. With less fluid in the blood, there is less volume for the heart to pump through the body, causing the heart to beat faster in an effort to get enough blood to the organs. The end result can be failure of multiple organs. These chemicals also are parts of cascades (chain reactions of proteins in the blood) that can result in blood clotting, as mentioned earlier. The blood-clotting cascade normally occurs following an injury to the **epithelium**. Its occurrence within the capillaries is abnormal. Scientists hypothesize that DIC is largely responsible for the hemorrhagic manifestation of filoviruses. The viral proteins that contribute to this manifestation are discussed next.

THE ROLE OF VIRAL PROTEINS

As mentioned earlier, the filovirus genome encodes seven proteins. One protein that has been the subject of much study is the filovirus glycoprotein. It is thought to play an important role in the **pathogenesis** (origin and development) of disease.

There are actually two slightly different glycoproteins, encoded by the same gene. Three hundred **amino acids** (the building blocks of proteins) are the same, but due to an editing process during transcription of the virus, two unique proteins are made. One protein, called the envelope glycoprotein, becomes a structural protein in the virus. It remains in the **viral envelope** (the outermost portion of the virus; see Figure 4.1). Here, one function of this protein is to bind to host cells, so the virus can enter and replicate within. The other form of protein is a **secreted** version, meaning it is released from infected cells. Both of these proteins have been shown experimentally to play a role in pathogenesis of infection. When the filovirus glycoprotein is expressed in infected cells, cell rounding is observed. This means that the cells are "sick" due to presence of the glycoprotein. Scientists have also observed differences in the **cytotoxicity** (ability to cause toxic damage to infected cells) in experiments using different types of Ebola virus. Expression of the Ebola Zaire glycoprotein in infected cells resulted in toxic effects in both human and nonhuman primate cells. Expression of the Ebola Reston glycoprotein only caused these effects

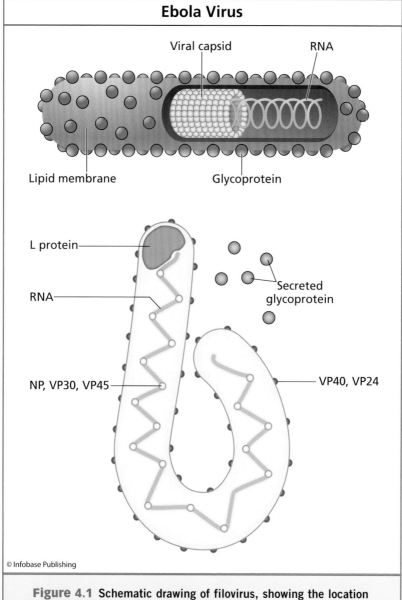

Ebola Virus

Viral capsid   RNA

Lipid membrane   Glycoprotein

L protein

RNA

Secreted glycoprotein

NP, VP30, VP45   VP40, VP24

© Infobase Publishing

Figure 4.1 Schematic drawing of filovirus, showing the location of the various proteins encoded by the virus.

in the cells derived from nonhuman primates. This may be one reason why the Ebola Reston strain has not been found to cause any clinical disease in humans, but is highly lethal in other primates. Another filovirus protein, VP40, is also cytotoxic, although less is known about the mechanism(s) by which this protein contributes to viral pathogenicity.

The secreted form of the glycoprotein may also play a role in suppressing the **immune response** to filovirus infection. Filoviruses destroy the immune system. As a result, patients infected with filoviruses are often unable to develop an adequate immune response to fight the infection. This is partly due to the fact that the virus infects some cells that play important roles in the development of an immune response. By infecting and destroying these cells, the virus renders the host unable to adequately fight the infection.

In addition, the presence of antibodies directed against the filovirus glycoprotein may actually enhance a filovirus infection. Animal models have shown that immunization with Ebola Zaire glycoprotein actually enhanced the infectivity of the virus. When scientists examined these models with Ebola Reston glycoprotein, the effect was much smaller. Again, this is another possible explanation for the difference in human fatalities between the two virus types. This information also has implications for the development of a vaccine based on the glycoprotein and for passive antibody transfer to infected patients.

Other filovirus proteins have also been implicated in directly affecting viral pathogenesis. A protein called VP35 has been shown to act as an **interferon** antagonist. Interferon is a protein of the host immune system that acts specifically in defense against viruses. Scientists hypothesize that the VP35 proteins may differ among types of Ebola as well, and that these differences may play a role in the differing lethality among these viral types. Indeed, a recent study showed that the VP35 protein from an Ebola Zaire virus, when coupled with a different protein (the L protein) from Ebola Reston, was unable to replicate. Though this does not address the difference in virulence between the two subtypes, it shows

EBOLA AND EDGAR ALLAN POE?

The "Red Death" had long devastated the country. No pestilence had ever been so fatal, or so hideous. Blood was its Avatar and its seal—the redness and the horror of blood. There were sharp pains, and sudden dizziness, and then profuse bleeding at the pores, with dissolution. The scarlet stains upon the body and especially upon the face of the victim, were the pest ban which shut him out from the aid and from the sympathy of his fellow-men. And the whole seizure, progress and termination of the disease, were the incidents of half an hour.

So opens Edgar Allen Poe's 1842 short story, "The Masque of the Red Death." In this tale, a fatal disease (the Red Death) has ravaged the land. To save himself, Prince Prospero shuts himself and a thousand noblemen in an abbey for six months, taking provisions to "bid defiance to contagion." After being shut in the abbey for so long, the prince decides to host a masquerade ball, even "while the pestilence raged most furiously abroad, that the Prince Prospero entertained his thousand friends at a masked ball of the most unusual magnificence." A visitor comes to the ball—impossible, since the abbey was strongly fortified:

that the VP35 proteins are divergent enough to affect human cells differently.

TRANSMISSION

Filoviruses are transmitted through contact with the blood or bodily fluids of infected patients or animals. In an outbreak situation, scientists have suggested that it may also be transmitted through similar contact with infected primates. The risk of

A strong and lofty wall girdled it in. This wall had gates of iron. The courtiers, having entered, brought furnaces and massy hammers and welded the bolts. They resolved to leave means neither of ingress or egress to the sudden impulses of despair or of frenzy from within.

The noblemen soon realize their visitor is none other than the Red Death itself, and within the span of a half an hour, all are dead within the abbey.

Is this "Red Death" modeled after a disease Poe had seen? The image of "severe bleeding at the pores" certainly seems compatible with a hemorrhagic fever disease. The other symptoms—sharp pains and dizziness—are also seen with Ebola. In the story, the townspeople also realize that the disease is contagious, since when they see a victim they "shut him out from the aid" of his countrymen. It is possible Poe loosely based the Red Death on yellow fever, which caused a large outbreak in 1841 in the United States. However, jaundice (the yellowing of the skin of the infected individual) is a notable symptom of that disease, and one that is not mentioned in Poe's tale. Perhaps Ebola is simply a disease that finally caught up with Poe's vivid imagination.

transmission is higher when the infected patient is in the later stages of illness, because **viremia** (the presence of virus in the blood) is higher at these stages. In a hospital setting, the reuse of unsterilized needles and syringes and the lack of barrier nursing procedures (such as masks, gowns, and gloves) were important factors in the spread of disease. Family members became infected due to close contact via bare skin, either in a hospital or a home setting. Family members often became infected while preparing the corpse of an infected loved one, as cultural traditions in Africa require the ritual cleansing of the body of relatives. Ebola has also been found to replicate at high levels in the skin. Contact with bodily fluids is likely not necessary to contract the virus. It is not completely clear, however, how the virus enters the body. Scientists hypothesize that the most likely entry route is via contact of contaminated fingers with either the eyes or the mouth. In some cases, airborne transmission may occur. This mode of transmission has been suggested in epidemiologic studies but has not been conclusively documented between humans. This is especially suspected with the Reston type, although in several cases of Ebola Zaire, there was no direct contact with an infected patient. In addition, Ebola virus was isolated from lung tissue during the 1995 Kikwit outbreak in the Democratic Republic of the Congo. It is not known, however, whether this was the primary route of infection. Sexual transmission is possible, as well, as the virus has been isolated from both vaginal and seminal fluids.

Convalescence (the process of recovering from infection) is a lengthy process, and virus has been isolated from patients as long as 82 days after onset of the disease. It is not known to what extent convalescent patients contribute to transmission of the virus.

5

Ecology of the Viruses

Janet [not her real name], a Colorado native, had saved up for over a year in order to take the vacation of a lifetime: a two-week safari in Uganda. She planned to camp, view exotic wildlife and African villages, and do some white-water rafting while she was there: essentially, spending several weeks just communing with nature in a far-off land. However, upon her return to the United States on New Year's Day 2008, she wasn't feeling well. Several days later, she went to her doctor complaining of a severe headache, chills, nausea, vomiting, and diarrhea. Thinking it was simple "traveler's diarrhea," her physician gave her a prescription for an antibiotic and sent her home. Still not feeling well four days later, and with a rash, severe weakness, and general confusion added to her list of symptoms, she returned to the doctor. Additional tests were done, and it was found that she now was suffering from hepatitis and renal failure, both very serious conditions. This time, she was admitted to the hospital for treatment and observation.

At this time, her doctors tested for a number of potential infections: leptospirosis, viral hepatitis, malaria, arboviral infection, acute schistosomiasis, rickettsial infection, and viral hemorrhagic fever viruses (including Marburg and Ebola hemorrhagic fever). All tests came back negative at this time. Janet was released after spending 10 days in the hospital and receiving a blood transfusion for her anemia. She still didn't have a diagnosis of her illness.

In June of that year, Janet read of a Marburg virus death in a Dutch tourist, who had happened to visit the same cave Janet had during her trip—Python's Cave in Uganda. Janet had visited the cave 10 days before she began feeling sick, and had noted bats flying above in the cave, and bat guano on the cave walls that she had touched. Janet asked that she be re-tested for Marburg. This time, her sample came back positive for Marburg antibodies, meaning she had indeed been infected with the virus. Her case made history as the first imported case of a filoviral hemorrhagic fever in the United States.[1]

The **ecology** of an organism refers to the study of its natural environment and its interaction with both its environment and other organisms within that environment. A study of the ecology of a pathogen seeks to answer the following questions:

- Where does the pathogen reside in nature?

- What is the host species?

- How is the pathogen transmitted to other individuals?

- What interactions does it have with other organisms, including other microbes?

- What is the **genetic diversity** (the amount of variation at the DNA level) of the species?

- Are particular **strains** or subtypes of the pathogen circulating that may be more common (or, perhaps, more virulent) than others?

- Are some types of the pathogen limited to certain geographical areas? What are the interactions of the pathogen with its reservoir host, if one exists?

- Do any other organisms (animals or even insects) play a role in the maintenance of the pathogen?

Scientists are still looking for answers to all of these questions regarding Ebola and Marburg.

CLUES FROM THE VIRUSES
The actual genetic sequence of filoviruses can provide clues to pieces of their ecology and epidemiology. With Ebola, the follow-

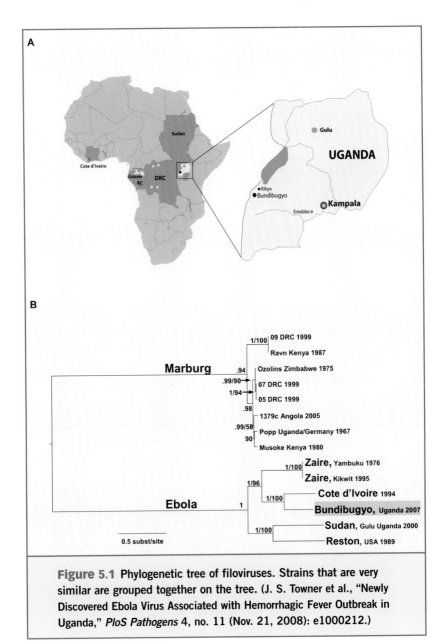

Figure 5.1 Phylogenetic tree of filoviruses. Strains that are very similar are grouped together on the tree. (J. S. Towner et al., "Newly Discovered Ebola Virus Associated with Hemorrhagic Fever Outbreak in Uganda," *PloS Pathogens* 4, no. 11 (Nov. 21, 2008): e1000212.)

ing subtypes have been identified: Ebola Zaire (EBO-Z), Ebola Sudan (EBO-S), Ebola Reston (EBO-R), Ebola Côte d'Ivorie (EBO-CI), and Ebola Bundibugyo (EBO-B). Scientists have found EBO-R in pigs and monkeys in the Philippines, and have recovered it from monkeys imported from that country into the United States and Europe. Serological studies have shown that Ebola viruses are circulating in parts of Asia and Madagascar, as well as in Central Africa and Western Africa. Most cases of Ebola and most seroprevalence (antibody evidence of prior infection) occur in areas of rain forest, although cases have also occurred in areas of more **savannah**-like ecology, such as those in Sudan and Uganda.

Looking at Ebola's **phylogenetic tree** (Figure 5.1), Ebola Reston and Ebola Zaire are the most divergent viruses; that is,

IS EBOLA TRANSMITTED BY ARTHROPODS?

Scientists do not know whether Ebola is airborne or whether it is transmitted by intermediate **vectors** in the wild. A vector is an intermediate host, such as an **arthropod**, which carries the pathogen from the reservoir host to the susceptible victim. Viruses such as yellow fever and dengue, both of which also can cause hemorrhagic fevers, are transmitted via arthropod vectors. In the case of those viruses, mosquitoes carry and transmit the diseases.

Several lines of evidence point to the possibility of insect vectors playing a role in the transmission of Ebola viruses in the wild. First is the relative conservation in nucleotide sequence of the Ebola virus. Subtypes of viruses remain fairly stable at the nucleotide level, even when viruses are compared that were isolated from cases that occurred years or even decades apart. Such stability is characteristic of pathogens that are maintained in more than one host, as selection pressures are strong to maintain proteins that may be necessary for binding in each host.

A second line of evidence rests in the fact that Ebola does not appear to be easily transmitted via direct contact. The

the ones most distantly related to one another. One can also see that the strain of Ebola that caused the 1976 outbreak in the Democratic Republic of the Congo (then known as Zaire) is very closely related to the strains found in the Congo in 1995 and in Gabon in 1994 and 1996. This was somewhat surprising, because Ebola is an RNA virus, and RNA viruses are often prone to errors in transcription ("copying" errors that occur when the virus reproduces). When an RNA virus is that stable in nature, it generally means that there is some kind of external constraint on its evolution, possibly due to pathogen-host coevolution. If the pathogen mutates too much, it may not be able to live in its

most efficient transmission of the virus occurs when needles are used (and, specifically, when dirty needles are reused). This may be similar to a natural inoculation via mosquito or other arthropod bite. Other viruses that are typically arthropod-borne show a similar inefficient transmission via direct contact or through the air.

Scientists have carried out a few studies to test the hypothesis that Ebola may be transmitted by arthropods. One study attempted to grow Ebola virus (Reston subtype) in mosquitoes and ticks, with no success. Other investigations, however, have shown that Marburg can survive in some species of mosquitoes for as long as three weeks even without replication. Thus, even if the virus may not successfully replicate in the arthropod, anthropods may act as natural "dirty needles" and transmit the virus between hosts in this manner. In addition, many arthropods have not been tested in order to determine if Ebola can grow within them or not. As is the case with so many aspects of Ebola ecology, transmission by arthropods remains an unknown factor.

natural host any longer. Mutations in the genome may lead it to cause disease in the host, or may mutate a protein necessary for binding to host cells, for instance. The stability of the Ebola virus suggests that there is something keeping Ebola subtypes distinct.

Despite years of study, the ecology of filoviruses remains unclear. The sporadic nature of outbreaks and their occurrence in remote areas of Africa lacking established medical research capabilities, and often in countries experiencing governmental strife and instability, compound the difficulty of determining the ecology of this particular virus. Often, the primary case, the first person in an outbreak known to be infected—and who likely acquired the virus from its wild reservoir—has died before questions could be answered regarding his or her previous whereabouts, diet, and other activities. It is difficult to determine where the patient could have contracted the disease. Seasonality may also play a role in the ecology of this disease. Many outbreaks have occurred during the rainy season. A search for the virus conducted during the dry season (as many ecological surveys have been) may miss key pieces of the puzzle of filovirus ecology. Nevertheless, scientists have attempted to make the most of outbreaks when they occur. They have undertaken studies between outbreaks in order to determine where the virus "hides" when it is not infecting humans. Scientists are also trying to find out how the virus moves from where it is maintained in nature into human populations. Perhaps, it is simply airborne. Maybe it is transmitted from butchering infected animals. It may also be transmitted by an intermediary such as an insect vector. The answer to these questions, despite years of investigation, remains unknown.

WHAT IS THE RESERVOIR OF EBOLA AND MARBURG VIRUSES?

One key missing piece of data regarding filovirus infection is the reservoir. A reservoir is the source of an infectious agent, the place where the agent is maintained and replicates. Non-human primates have been suggested as a reservoir of this virus, based on several lines of evidence, including the fact that several outbreaks of Ebola have been traced to contact with nonhuman primates, and the discovery that a fair number of nonhuman primates can survive infection, as shown by serological studies. The fact that Ebola infection is highly lethal in most nonhuman primate species suggests that it is unlikely that these primates are the true reservoir. In all likelihood, they are occasionally infected, as are humans. Despite several large studies, scientists have yet to discover the true reservoir of filoviruses in nature.

In 1976, simultaneous outbreaks of Ebola hemorrhagic fever occurred in Sudan and the Democratic Republic of the Congo. An analysis of the viruses causing these outbreaks showed that there were two subtypes of the Ebola virus, designated Ebola Sudan and Ebola Zaire. Scientists conducted investigations in both locations, in an effort to determine the ecology of the viruses causing these outbreaks. In the Democratic Republic of the Congo, more than 800 bedbugs and 147 mammal species (mostly wild rodents) were collected for investigation. Scientists tested all samples to determine if they were positive for the Ebola virus, but no virus was found in any of the insects or the animals. A group of investigators later narrowed down a list of additional mammals to test based on size, susceptibility to Ebola infection in the lab, known habitat, and frequency of contact with humans. These mammals may serve as targets of future ecological surveys in the search for a reservoir.

The Sudan outbreak was traced back to individuals working in a warehouse where cotton was stored. The warehouse was infested with bats, an interesting connection for scientists. Kitum Cave in Kenya was also bat-infested, and visitors there had contracted the Marburg virus. Were bats the reservoir of filoviruses? To examine this hypothesis, scientists tested 100 vertebrate specimens (including bats) for the Ebola virus the following year. None of them was found to be positive. Despite a large effort on the part of researchers, the reservoir of Ebola was not found.

Scientists used 1,664 animals, mainly small rodents, when they conducted another large-scale serological study in 1979–1980 in Cameroon and the Democratic Republic of the Congo.

Figure 5.2 Egyptian fruit bats (*Rousettus aegypticus*), a widespread African fruit bat, which has recently been linked to Marburg virus as a possible vector for transmission of the disease. (© Tom McHugh/ Photo Researchers, Inc.)

Again, no virus was detected. A number of flaws, however, were noted in the study. The animals captured included an over-representation of animals that were common to settlements (**peridomestic** animals). Because Ebola virus infection is such a rare event, the reservoir is unlikely to be a common residential animal. In addition, much better and more sensitive tests have been developed since this study was undertaken. These newer tests may capture positive samples that the older tests missed.

Following the 1995 outbreak in Kikwit, in the Democratic Republic of the Congo, scientists conducted yet another ecologic survey. Again, however, seasonality was a factor. The study team arrived in June 1995, but the primary case had become infected in December 1994. Nevertheless, a team collected samples to test for the Ebola virus. In this study, scientists collected 3,066 specimens from a total of 6 sites (they also purchased large animals from hunters). Most of the samples were small mammals, although they collected birds, reptiles, and amphibians, as well. Scientists collected more than 34,000 arthropods. Most of these were mosquitoes, bedbugs, and ticks. Once again, despite testing almost 40,000 specimens, scientists were unable to isolate the virus, and they did not find any serologic evidence of previous infection. The reservoir remained, and still remains, unknown, despite years of work on the part of researchers and many thousands of dollars spent to uncover it.

An interesting and novel hypothesis involves the possibility of plants as the reservoir of the Ebola virus. Several lines of reasoning support this idea. For one, Ebola is generally quite pathogenic in vertebrates, killing them quickly rather than allowing for persistence of the virus. Thus, the virus does not appear to be well adapted for infection in most vertebrate species, and it is possible therefore that the host of the virus is a non-vertebrate species. The appearance of Ebola outbreaks may occur at a similar time as the flowering of a plant. Additionally, a virus that appears to be similar to filoviruses was isolated from a leafhopper (*Psammotettix* species) from France. Again, this is an intriguing idea, but no evidence has yet been found to implicate plants as playing a role in Ebola infection.

EVIDENCE OF INFECTION IN NONHUMAN PRIMATES

Just as several intensive research studies have targeted insects and small animals, scientists have also carried out a number of studies to look at evidence of previous Ebola infection in larger primates and in humans in Africa. A 15-year survey was conducted in Cameroon, Gabon, and the Democratic Republic of the Congo between 1985 and 2000. The researchers tested a total of 790 nonhuman primates of 20 different species. Several studies had previously suggested that human outbreaks of Ebola often occurred simultaneously with outbreaks in chimpanzees. In other cases, infection with Ebola had been traced back to the butchering of a wild chimpanzee, or in the case of the Ivory Coast case, to the necropsy of a chimp that had died in the wild, presumably of Ebola infection. In this study, in contrast, many isolates were found to be positive for antibody to the Ebola virus. This means that these animals had been exposed to the Ebola virus, and had survived the infection. The highest **sero-prevalence** was found in chimpanzees in Cameroon, where almost 18% (21 out of 119 tested) were positive for antibody to the Ebola virus. Other species found to be positive included gorillas and baboons. Of note was the finding that none of the captive-born animals tested positive for Ebola virus antibody, suggesting that these animals were exposed to virus circulating naturally in the wild in those areas of Africa.

While scientists continue to speculate about a reservoir of Ebola, the virus is decimating the great apes in Central Africa. **Primatologists** (scientists who study primates) and local villagers noted a large increase in the number of animal carcasses found in forested areas before and during the 2001 Ebola outbreaks in Gabon. The discovery of carcasses is normally a rare event. Most primates are killed by predators, and decomposition is rapid due to the warm, humid environment. Over an 8-month period, a team of investigators learned of at least 64 animal carcasses in Gabon, most of them gorillas. The researchers hypothesized that thousands of gorillas may have died from Ebola infection during this outbreak. Following this outbreak, sightings of both gorillas and chimpanzees in the area decreased significantly. In fact, gorilla sightings (or other evidence of their presence, including dung and trails) decreased by 50%. Chimpanzee sightings decreased by 88%, suggesting a severe population decline in both species. Other evidence supports these observations. Eight groups of gorillas (totaling 143 individuals) that had been monitored by primatologists for 10 years disappeared sometime between October 2002 and January 2003. A similar occurrence in the Taï Forest of Côte d'Ivoire in 1994 coincided with the discovery of Ebola in that area of Africa. Sequencing of the Ebola viruses isolated from some of the carcasses suggested that the deaths were due to multiple introductions of the virus, rather than one continuous epidemic. It is therefore likely that these apes were encountering the natural reservoir of Ebola somewhere in their habitat.

Chimpanzees have been affected in the Ivory Coast as well. A 1994 study of chimpanzees in this area (that led to the identification of the Ebola Côte d'Ivoire subtype) identified an ongoing outbreak, which had been linked to eating the meat of a red colobus monkey (species *Colobus badius badius*). It was estimated that approximately 25% of a community of 43 chimpanzees was decimated by the outbreak.

Primatologists are conflicted about what, if anything, should be done to halt the spread of disease. They are unsure whether some apes should be moved to other areas, which may be free from Ebola, or whether they should be left alone. One thing that researchers do agree upon is that the **poaching** (illegal hunting) of gorillas in these areas needs to be stopped. Scientist William Karesh of the Wildlife Conservation Society in New York City stated, "Let's take what we do know—that people can get this disease from eating infected primates—and use that to do something we know will protect the great apes." For now, that may be all we are able to do (Figure 5.3).

BATS AS FILOVIRUS RESERVOIR

Bats have been associated with filovirus infection since the infection was initially discovered (Figure 5.2). In 1976, *Tadarida (mops) trevori*, a species of bats, were found in the roof of the N'zara cotton factory in Sudan. During that outbreak, the index case and two other early cases had worked at this factory. Ebola reappeared in this same location in 1979. Again in this outbreak, the index case was a worker at the N'zara cotton factory. In addition, bats have been linked to cases of Marburg virus, a filovirus closely related to Ebola. Two cases of Marburg have been linked to a cave on Mount Elgon in Kenya. This cave was home to thousands of bats. In addition, experimental evidence has shown that bats of the *Tadarida* genus can be infected with Ebola in the laboratory, and transmit it through their **guano** (excrement). However, in early studies, none of the bats that had been captured during ecological surveys tested positive for the Ebola virus. Additionally, strains of Ebola that have been experimentally tested in other members of the *Tadarida* genus were found to be highly pathogenic. A characteristic of a reservoir species is that the pathogen generally causes little or no harm in the reservoir; thus, it would be expected that infection with Ebola in this species would be **asymptomatic** (causing no symptoms of infection).

In the past several years, the evidence has mounted that bats do indeed play a critical role in the maintenance and transmission of filoviruses in Africa. A 2005 study examined over 1,000 animals in central Africa, including 679 bats. These animals were tested for Ebola virus infection in multiple ways, including antibody and nucleic acid detection methods. Three different species of fruit bats were found to be positive for Ebola virus: *Hypsignathus monstrosus*, *Epomops franqueti*, and *Myonycteris torquata*. Each of these species has a broad range across Africa, which includes regions that have previously experienced Ebola outbreaks. This paper was the first to find evidence of filovirus-infected bats in the wild, and suggested

Figure 5.3 Great apes in Africa, including gorillas and chimpanzees, are in danger due to the Ebola virus, which has severely depleted their populations in many areas of the continent. (© AP Images)

that fruit bats may spread the virus to primates via several different routes. Humans or other primates may eat the fruit bats, becoming infected directly via contact with bat secretions, or the bats may contaminate fruit which is consumed by humans or other primates (including gorillas).

While only Ebola infection was examined in this study, a 2007 paper found Marburg virus in another fruit bat species, *Rousettus aegyptiacus*. These bats were collected from the countries of Gabon and Republic of Congo in Africa, providing further evidence that bats could play a role as reservoir species.

Finally, while these publications are suggestive of bat-to-human transmission of filoviruses, they certainly do not prove it. However, other recent research has started to fill this gap, describing an outbreak of Ebola in the Democratic Republic of Congo that was linked to the mass migration of fruit bats (*H. monstrosus*). These bats migrate in huge numbers through villages in the DRC in the spring, when they are hunted by people in the villages along the migration paths. The hunters both consume these bats themselves, and also sell excess at markets. One village inhabitant became ill after purchasing one of these bats. Though he only had a fairly mild infection and survived, he infected his 4-year-old daughter, who rapidly died from the infection. In keeping with local tradition, her female relatives and friends of the family prepared her for burial. One of these women subsequently became ill, and infected several others, starting the outbreak which resulted in up to 264 cases and 186 deaths. This was the first outbreak which investigators were able to trace back to a confirmed bat contact.[2]

EVIDENCE OF INFECTION IN HUMANS

Scientists have conducted studies to examine the prevalence of human exposure to Ebola in Africa. A 1983 survey in Cameroon used **indirect fluorescence assay**. Among 1,517 apparently healthy people with no history of hemorrhagic fever disease, 9.7% were found to have antibodies to Ebola virus. In this study, the highest rates of seropositivity were found among Pygmies (groups of African forest dwellers), young adults, and rain forest farmers. Another study looked at all filoviruses in Central

Africa (Marburg and Ebola). Again, a higher positive rate for the Ebola virus was found among Pygmies than among non-Pygmies, but no statistically significant difference was found between the two groups; thus, the small differences found between the groups may have been due to chance rather than biology. Scientists conducted more research during the 1995 outbreak in the Democratic Republic of the Congo. There was a surprisingly high seroprevalence of the virus in West Africa and Central Africa. Thus, similar to the situation with the Ebola Reston virus, it appears that there must be types of Ebola circulating in Africa that cause **subclinical** disease (disease without symptoms). In addition, a higher percentage of rural dwellers than city dwellers was found to possess antibodies to Ebola. In a separate study, scientists found a higher seroprevalence rate among hunters versus farmers, further suggesting that the reservoir of Ebola lies somewhere in the African forests.

6

Methods of Detection and Treatment

Historically, scientists have measured infection with filoviruses using tests that detect antibodies to the virus. In fact, scientists use several different tests, with varying degrees of **sensitivity** (ability to correctly identify positive samples) and **specificity** (ability to correctly identify negative samples). One common test is called the indirect fluorescence assay (IFA). A schematic of this test is shown in Figure 6.1. In short, scientists apply cells known to be infected with the Ebola virus to a slide. They then add **serum** (the liquid portion of the blood, which contains antibodies) from a suspected patient and allow it to dry. This is the primary antibody. Next, they add a secondary antibody, which will specifically recognize the human antibodies. This secondary antibody (which is often derived from goats) is **conjugated** (linked) to a protein called **fluorescein**. When antibodies to Ebola or Marburg are present in the patient's sample, they will bind to the virus or virus particles on the slide. The fluorescein-labeled secondary antibody will then bind to the primary antibodies. Scientists then view the slide under a fluorescent microscope. Samples that are positive will glow a bright green or yellow color (see Figure 6.2).

One problem with IFA, however, is the fact that both its sensitivity and its specificity are fairly low. Therefore, the test may miss samples that are positive, and may incorrectly identify samples that are negative (these are called "false negatives" and "false positives," respectively). Other tests are based on the same principle of antigen, primary antibody, and secondary

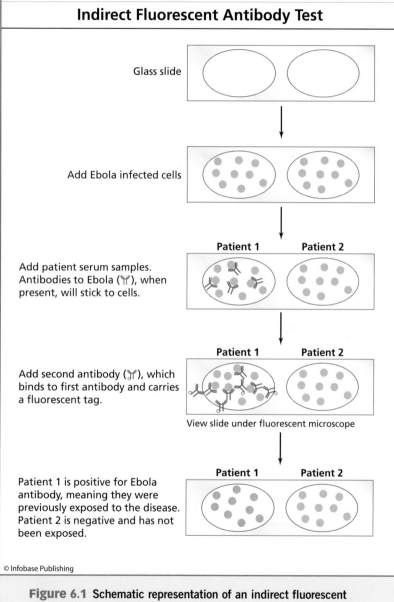

Figure 6.1 Schematic representation of an indirect fluorescent antibody test for detection of antibodies to certain agents (in this example, Ebola virus).

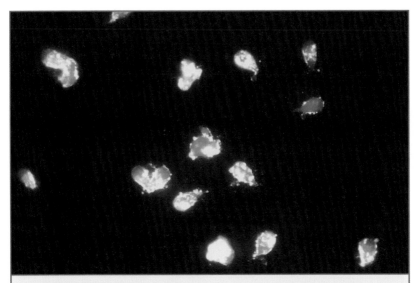

Figure 6.2 Indirect fluorescent antibody test. A positive sample (one that contains antibody against the target organism, such as the Ebola virus) will bind to infected cells on the glass slide. The secondary antibody, coupled with a protein fluorescein, will attach to the primary antibody, and will fluoresce under ultraviolet light as seen in this figure. (Centers for Disease Control and Prevention)

antibody. However, the type of protein that is conjugated to the secondary antibody, the method of development, and visualization of results differ.

Scientists also use **ELISA (enzyme-linked immunosorbant assay)**, another test, to diagnose previous infection with filoviruses. In this test, scientists place viral **antigens** (viral proteins that are recognized by the host immune system) in tiny plastic wells and allow them to dry. Similar to the IFA, they then apply sera from patients, before a secondary antibody is applied. In this case, however, this secondary antibody is often coupled to a molecule called horseradish peroxidase. Scientists then add a **substrate** (in this situation, a chemical that would interact with the horseradish peroxidase) containing a colored dye coupled with peroxide. The peroxidase **cleaves** (cuts) the substrate, resulting in the release of colored molecules. The intensity of color correlates to the amount of antibody that is present in the serum. The darker the color, the higher the level of antibody present. ELISA is more sensitive and specific than IFA, but because a special reader is necessary to determine the results, it is a more difficult test to carry out in the field.

These tests can also be used to distinguish between a current or very recent infection and a past infection. The human body produces several different types of antibodies (technically called **immunoglobulins**, abbreviated Ig). These different types are known as IgG, IgM, IgA, IgE, and IgD. The most important antibodies for diagnosing Ebola are IgM and IgG. If a secondary antibody specific to human IgM is used, a current or very recent Ebola infection can be detected. IgM is the first type of antibody that the body produces. As the immune response progresses, the body switches from producing IgM to producing IgG.

Scientists recently developed a new immunological test for filoviral infection. Rather than using patient sera, this test uses skin samples from patients suspected of infection. Skin samples are placed in a chemical called formalin. This kills the viruses, making the samples safe to work with in the absence of **biosafety level 4** (**BSL-4**) facilities. The general procedure, however, is quite similar to the assays previously described.

PCR-BASED METHODS OF DETECTION

Immunological methods are most useful for detecting past infection with the Ebola or Marburg viruses. They can detect current infection as well, but there are some problems with this. Filovirus infection itself has an immunosuppressive effect. This means that patients with a current infection may not be producing antibodies. A test to detect these specific antibodies will be negative, even when the patient is, indeed, infected with a filovirus. In addition, an antibody response is not immediate. Detectable levels of IgM take several days to develop. A test performed too soon may appear falsely negative. An IgG response takes even longer. It can take two weeks or longer for a patient to produce enough IgG to detect in an IFA or ELISA.

PCR (polymerase chain reaction)–based tests eliminate the antibodies. These tests directly detect the presence of virus nucleic acid in blood or tissues. Whether the host produces an immune response or not is irrelevant. This assay is both highly sensitive and specific. There are shortcomings, however, with this technique as well. Filoviruses are RNA viruses, and RNA is an unstable molecule that degrades rapidly if not handled correctly. Even proteins on our hands (called **RNAses**) can destroy any RNA that may be present in a sample. In a field environment, such as rural Africa, material handling obviously poses a problem.

While degradation of the sample RNA may produce a false negative result, false positives are possible due to sample contamination. PCR is a very sensitive procedure. Essentially, the amount of virus RNA present in a sample is doubled during each cycle. Typically, there are 30 to 40 cycles in a run. Therefore, the gene being amplified by PCR will double in amount 30 to 40 times. If even a miniscule amount of contamination is present—as little as just a few viral particles carried into the sample by the air or present on a contaminated glove or counter top, these will be amplified in the reaction—thus producing a false positive result. Therefore, precautions need to be taken to minimize this contamination. Once again, specialized machines and chemicals are necessary to carry out this procedure, making it difficult to perform in rural areas.

METAGENOMICS

A newer molecular method that has been employed for filovirus detection is called metagenomics. In this technique, rather than simply looking for virus-specific gene segments, the entire genome of a sample is sequenced. For example, a patient blood sample may be taken and sequenced, which would include the host genome sequence (from the blood cells present) and also

Polymerase Chain Reaction

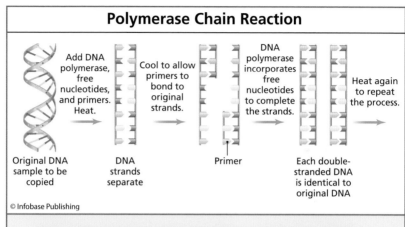

Add DNA polymerase, free nucleotides, and primers. Heat.

Cool to allow primers to bond to original strands.

DNA polymerase incorporates free nucleotides to complete the strands.

Heat again to repeat the process.

Original DNA sample to be copied

DNA strands separate

Primer

Each double-stranded DNA is identical to original DNA

© Infobase Publishing

Figure 6.3 Schematic of the polymerase chain reaction (PCR), a procedure by which filovirus RNA can be amplified to allow for identification.

any infectious agents present in the blood. The host DNA can then be identified and eliminated from further analysis, leaving behind any remaining virus sequences. This method was used to find the newest Ebola subtype, Bundibugyo.

TREATMENT

Treatment strategies for filovirus infections generally fall into two groups: passive transfer of immunoglobulin (antibody) and chemical **antivirals** (drugs that prevent replication of the virus). Both have had varied degrees of success.

In the early stages of Ebola infection, scientists administer serum from patients who have recovered from the disease (convalescent patients). Despite a few small-scale trials, it is still not known whether this is a beneficial treatment. Antibody directed against the Ebola virus is not neutralizing. It does not bind to the virus and target it for elimination by the host's immune system. Nevertheless, scientists have conducted several studies in order to determine if passive antibody transfer has any benefit in the treatment of Ebola.

TAQ POLYMERASE AND PCR

Taq polymerase began as a relatively obscure discovery in 1976. It is a **polymerase** (a protein that functions to link nucleic acids together) derived from a bacterium called *Thermus aquaticus*. ("*Taq*" comes from the first letters of its genus and species names). This bacterium was isolated from a hot spring, and is classified as a **thermophile** (it thrives in very hot environments). As such, the bacterium needs to have enzymes that carry out its day-to-day metabolic needs, but still function at very high temperatures (near or above the boiling point of water, a temperature at which most proteins would be rendered nonfunctional).

Nearly a decade later, scientist Kary Mullis introduced a technique called the polymerase chain reaction (PCR), using *Taq* polymerase. Using *Taq*, free nucleotides, small pieces of deoxyribonucleic acid (DNA) to serve as **primers**, and a DNA sample to serve as a **template**, millions of copies of a piece of DNA could be made. This procedure has revolutionized all fields of biology, and is used in genetic research, medicine, and even forensic science.

Scientists used convalescent serum, along with an antiviral protein called human interferon, in the case of four laboratory workers in Russia who had been exposed to the virus. The lab workers survived, but because there was no **control group** (a group of patients with a similar infection, who did not receive treatment), it is not known whether their survival was a result of the serum, the interferon, both of the treatments, or neither of the treatments.

Scientists used the same procedure during the 1995 outbreak in Kikwit in the Democratic Republic of the Congo. In June 1995, at the end of the epidemic, a total of eight patients were **transfused** with blood from patients who had recovered from the illness. Seven of these patients survived following this treatment. Once again, however, there was no good control group with which to compare the patients. Earlier in the epidemic, the fatality rate had been 80%, but by the end of the epidemic, the rate had declined due to the institution of barrier nursing procedures coupled with fewer new patients entering the hospital. In addition, simply providing proper nutrition and hydration in the latter part of the epidemic likely played a role in improving the survival rate.

Researchers undertook a controlled experimental approach to evaluating this treatment, using animal models (guinea pigs, mice, and cynomolgus monkeys) and equine (horse) antibody. Monkeys that were treated with antibody survived longer than those that were not treated. Eleven of 12 monkeys that received passive antibody eventually died, however, of Ebola. Similar results were obtained in mice, while all guinea pigs treated survived. Another group of researchers carried out a similar experiment using Ebola antibody obtained from sheep and goats. The antibody was tested in mice, baboons, and guinea pigs to see if it was effective in treating disease. Most animals survived in this experiment, but they received antibody treatment either before injection of Ebola, or up to two hours after infection. This time frame could not be replicated in an actual outbreak situation, because a patient often does not realize he or she has been infected until symptoms appear, and this usually occurs days or weeks following the initial infection. This treatment could, however, be useful for laboratory workers who have been bitten by an infected animal or accidentally stuck with an infected needle.

Clearly, scientists have much more work to do before they understand the basic biology of filoviruses, in order to treat the infections they cause. The work is dangerous and daunting, however, and we are lucky to have people willing to risk their lives both in the laboratory and in the field in order to better understand and treat this disease.

7

Developing a Vaccine

Fewer than 2,500 people have died from infection with Ebola since its discovery in 1976. Averaging out its mortality over a 40-year period, this amounts to a mortality of about .2 people per day. Forty-five hundred people worldwide die every day from tuberculosis. Thirty-six hundred people die each day from malaria. Five thousand people die every day from diarrheal diseases, and some 1,400 people die each day from influenza. Additionally, there has never been a case of Ebola in humans that originated in the United States. One cannot help but wonder why American scientists, using money obtained from American taxpayers, are working on a **vaccine** (suspensions of either dead or weakened pathogens, or products created by pathogens, designed to cause immunity to the pathogen in the host) to prevent this disease. In fact, there are a number of reasons for this.

Perhaps the main reason why an effective vaccine for Ebola is imperative comes from the outbreak in Reston, Virginia (see Chapter 3). As discussed, no human illness has resulted from the Reston strain of Ebola. The possibility of a mutation in the strain, however, which may change it from a harmless strain to a killer of humans is ever-present, and is certainly on the minds of researchers familiar with Ebola. We simply do not know enough about what causes pathogenicity in this virus to ever think we are safe, even when researching a strain that has not yet killed any human beings. An effective vaccine would go a long way toward alleviating this concern.

Another persistent fear among U.S. scientists is the movement and adaptation of viruses to new areas where they had not previously been known to exist. Pathogens that are either new to an area, or simply new to scientists, are termed emerging pathogens, and their numbers are increasing all the time. A recent example of a virus that has appeared in a new area and wreaked havoc on the population is the West Nile virus. This virus, previously recognized in the Middle East and Europe, was found in the eastern United States in 1999. Since that time, it has appeared throughout the United States, and has been found to cause serious disease in several species, including humans and horses. There is a fear this could happen with Ebola and Marburg as well. The mechanisms by which pathogens are able to enter and adapt to a new area are not known. Because we know so little about the ecology of filoviruses, we cannot predict with any accuracy whether the virus could ever become established in the United States.

International travel is another risk factor in the spread of the disease, and a compelling reason for the need to develop an effective vaccine against filoviruses. The incubation time for Ebola is approximately 2 to 21 days. It would certainly be possible for someone to be exposed to Ebola one day, hop on a plane, and be halfway around the world by the time he or she showed symptoms of the disease, several days to two weeks later. Because the initial symptoms of Ebola and Marburg resemble influenza and a host of other influenza-like illnesses, a diagnosis of Ebola would not likely be considered for someone showing these symptoms in New York City, for example. Luckily, the Ebola outbreaks identified thus far do not seem to be transmitted efficiently through the air, and simple barrier nursing procedures (such as wearing gloves and masks) coupled with safe needle use have proven effective at ending ongoing outbreaks. It is, therefore, unlikely that one case would trigger an outbreak in most countries with adequate medical services. There are no guarantees, however. For example, Ebola Reston is thought to be airborne, but scientists do not know exactly why this strain of the virus is able to be more efficiently transmitted through the air than other strains. If a traveler happened to be infected with a highly lethal strain of the virus that carried a mutation allowing airborne transmission, there would be no way to know what the outbreak would be like, particularly if it occurred in a large metropolitan area, or if the patient unknowingly transmitted the virus among the community before exhibiting symptoms. In a case such as this, a vaccine would be invaluable.

Finally, there is the possibility of a future outbreak of Ebola or Marburg that is not accidental. Attacks of biological terrorism are an unfortunate reality in our world, and a virus with the lethality of the Zaire strain of Ebola is an attractive option for terrorist groups. Scientists still have not developed an effective treatment for Ebola infection, so a vaccine would be the only

HEMORRHAGIC FEVER VIRUSES AS BIOLOGICAL WARFARE AGENTS

Hemorrhagic fever viruses are attractive possible biological warfare agents. They possess a number of qualities that make them appealing:

- the potential to cause high morbidity (illness) and mortality (death)

- the potential for person-to-person transmission

- a low infective dose (very few viral particles are necessary to cause infection)

- possibility of airborne transmission

- potential for large-scale production

- no available vaccine, or one in limited supply

- previous research and development as a biological weapon.

In addition, these viruses have the ability to cause widespread public fear and panic simply by the mention of their name or a description of their clinical symptoms. If an out-option if an airborne strain of Ebola were ever released by a terrorist group.

THE CHALLENGES

Though there are a number of important reasons for carrying out research in order to formulate a vaccine against filovirus infections, there are just as many, if not more, obstacles standing in the way. First and foremost is the simple difficulty of working with the viruses in the laboratory. Filoviruses are classified as biosafety level 4 (BSL-4) agents. This means scientists can only carry out experiments with the virus in special facilities,

break of Ebola were linked to a biological weapons attack in the United States, the public reaction would likely be intense. Fear and panic are often the goal of terrorists who launch such attacks.

This may seem far-fetched, but several hemorrhagic fever viruses (including Marburg and Ebola) have reportedly been weaponized by the former Soviet Union, the United States, and possibly North Korea. The Soviet Union is known to have continued its biological weapons program until at least 1992; the United States discontinued its program in 1969. Various terrorist groups worldwide have either worked to weaponize hemorrhagic fever viruses or have attempted to do so. The Japanese terrorist group Aum Shinrikyo released a nerve gas called sarin in a Japanese subway in March 1995, killing 11 people and injuring more than 5,500. This group sent agents to Africa in an attempt to obtain samples of Ebola to turn into biological weapons. This effort was unsuccessful, as far as we know, but no one can be sure that other groups have not succeeded where this one failed.

and the researchers need to be dressed in "space suits" and decontaminated (literally washed in chemicals to kill any virus that may remain on their suits) after leaving the laboratory (Figure 7.1). In addition, all the work is done in laboratories that are under negative air pressure. Air is always flowing into the room, and it only leaves via special devices called **HEPA filters**. The holes in these filters are too tiny even for the Ebola virus to pass through. Therefore, any filovirus that may become airborne in the lab will be trapped in these filters, rather than being released into the environment. The combined expense and difficulty of maintaining these laboratories serves to keep filoviruses contained to only a few facilities worldwide. More importantly, these measures help protect both the general public and the researchers who risk their lives to increase our understanding of this deadly virus.

Other difficulties revolve around the simple fact that despite much research, there are still many unanswered questions about filovirus pathogenesis. Because there have been so few human cases, scientists do not know which components of the immune response (the body's defense against pathogens) are most important in protection against infection. Researchers believe that a vaccine should activate specific **T cell** responses and induce an antibody response. T cells are a type of cell of the body's immune system that are generally most important in defense against viruses and other intracellular pathogens. Antibodies are proteins produced by another type of cell of the immune system, called **B cells**. These proteins specifically recognize parts of the invading pathogen and bind to it. This targets the pathogen for destruction and elimination by other cells of the immune system, including **phagocytes**, which engulf and destroy the invading pathogens.

One probelm in filovirus vaccine development, however, is the fact that we do not know which viral proteins should be targeted to most effectively prevent disease. In addition, there is

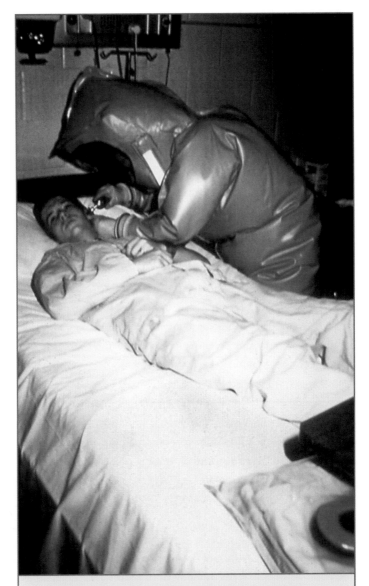

Figure 7.1 A researcher in a "space suit" examines an Ebola patient. Researchers must wear these protective suits to protect them from contamination by the virus. (Centers for Disease Control and Prevention)

no good animal model of disease. Generally, primate models are used, but different species of primates have different susceptibilities to infection with Ebola. This complicates the decision about which species best simulates a human infection. Other species have been used as models (including mice and guinea pigs), but again, it is difficult to directly extrapolate results from these experiments and apply them to what may happen in a human infection.

Finally, there are limits to the type of vaccine that can be used for filoviruses. Many common vaccines are a **live attenuated vaccine** or a **killed vaccine**. A live attenuated vaccine is one in which the virus is able to replicate within human cells, but has been changed in some manner so that it does not cause illness to the recipient. These often produce a stronger immune response than a killed vaccine. A killed vaccine is one in which the virus has been inactivated in some way, either via heat, chemicals, or radiation, so that it is unable to replicate or cause an infection in the host. Ebola and Marburg are much too lethal, however, to even consider a live attenuated vaccine. Because they are RNA viruses, the possibility of the attenuated virus mutating to become a lethal virus is simply too great. Even a killed virus is not a realistic option, as no vaccine facility exists with the BL-4 capabilities needed to manufacture and contain the virus prior to inactivation. These problems, and some possible solutions, are discussed below.

TYPES OF VACCINE

As is common in all aspects of filovirus research, scientists must "think outside the box" in order to formulate an effective vaccine for this virus. In spite of the numerous challenges, recent breakthroughs have brought the reality of an Ebola or Marburg vaccine closer to fruition.

As mentioned earlier, a number of traditional vaccine strategies simply will not work for filoviruses, due to the extremely deadly nature of the viruses. As such, new ideas have to be developed for vaccination. A team of researchers, led by

Gary Nabel, has tested a strategy in monkeys that appears to be highly protective and, most important, appears to work quickly. Previously tested Ebola vaccinations required up to six months to achieve full immunity, and required multiple **booster** (follow-up) injections to reach this goal.

Nabel's researchers used a unique strategy. They took the genes that encode the Ebola GP and NP proteins and stitched them into another virus—an **adenovirus**. Normally, adenoviruses cause minor illness, such as colds. In this case, the viruses were being used to expose the host immune system to the Ebola proteins, prompting the host to generate an immune response to the Ebola antigens. The researchers then injected this modified adenovirus into macaques. After four weeks, they injected these same monkeys with a lethal dose of Ebola virus. All monkeys that had received the vaccine survived, while the monkeys in the control group (which did not receive the vaccine) all died of Ebola infection. These findings were important. In the event of an Ebola outbreak, scientists could employ a strategy referred to as **ring vaccination**. The aim of ring vaccination is to contain an outbreak by first vaccinating all possible contacts of the detected cases. Next, all the contacts of *these* people are vaccinated, until all known contacts have been vaccinated, in an effort to stop the outbreak.

One potential problem with Nabel's vaccine is the fact that humans have been naturally exposed to many adenoviruses throughout their lifetime, creating a preexisting immunity to them. If someone is immune to the adenoviral vaccine vector, the virus will be unable to replicate and cause the host to generate immunity to the Ebola virus proteins it expresses. Researchers have proposed a way to circumvent this problem by using adenoviruses that are uncommon in the general population when (and if) a vaccine goes into production.

VACCINE PRODUCTION

Finally, it is not enough simply to have a vaccine that works. The vaccine must also be tested for safety, and someone must be willing to mass-produce it. A Dutch biotechnology company, Crucell, has offered to collaborate with the National Institute of Allergy and Infectious Diseases in the United States to further develop, and eventually produce, an Ebola virus vaccine. Clearly, this vaccine will not be added to the vaccinations children and adults receive on a regular basis. Indeed, the hope is that it will never be needed by the general population of the United States at all. It could, however, be administered to scientists who work with Ebola virus on a regular basis. Regardless of how it might eventually be used, having a stock of filovirus vaccine on hand in the event of an outbreak, either in this country or abroad, is a wise course of action.

8

Other Hemorrhagic Fevers

Though Ebola may be the best-known hemorrhagic fever, it is certainly not the only one, nor is it the most common. A number of other viruses cause symptoms similar to Ebola and Marburg, though none with the remarkable **fatality rate** seen with Ebola infection. These other hemorrhagic fever viruses will be briefly discussed here.

CRIMEAN-CONGO HEMORRHAGIC FEVER VIRUS (CCHF)

A **bunyavirus** is the cause of Crimean-Congo hemorrhagic fever, a tick-borne disease. Scientists discovered this disease in separate outbreaks in Russia and in the Democratic Republic of the Congo in the mid-twentieth century. Both outbreaks were recognized as being caused by the same virus in 1969. The virus can infect mammals, birds, and humans. *Hyalomma* ticks spread the disease, and function as a reservoir host as well. Though the tick may be infected by taking a blood meal from an infected animal, the virus can also be transmitted **transovarially**—via the egg from one generation to the next, so that the offspring are infected with the virus even before they emerge from their egg. This type of tick can be found throughout Eastern Europe, the Mediterranean, Western Asia, and Africa and is the primary source of the spread of the disease. As with Ebola and other hemorrhagic fever diseases, however, direct transmission is also possible as a result of contact with contaminated bodily fluids. Occupational exposure is common as well, especially among farmers and veterinarians.

In addition to ticks, many other animals also act as reservoirs for the virus, including cattle, sheep, goats, and hares.

The incubation period for the disease ranges from approximately two to nine days. Initial symptoms, including fever, headache, abdominal pain, and vomiting, are nonspecific and sometimes occur suddenly. These symptoms may be followed by a rash, sore throat, jaundice, and changes in mood. Hemorrhage is a late symptom. The fatality rate has varied among studies, ranging from as low as 15% to as high as 70%. Mild or unapparent infections can also occur. Serological studies have shown the presence of anti-CCHF virus antibodies in people who have not had clinical CCHF. Ribavirin may be used to treat this disease.

YELLOW FEVER

Yellow fever is a mosquito-borne member of the family *Flaviviridae*, genus *Flavivirus*, found in tropical areas of Africa and South America (Figure 8.1). In urban areas, humans serve as the reservoir host, while monkeys play this role in the jungle. In the jungle environment, humans can become accidentally infected but are not the preferred target of the mosquitoes (generally *Aedes aegypti*) that transmit the disease. Between 1948 and 2001, almost 40,000 cases of yellow fever were reported to the World Health Organization. More than 75% of cases occurred in Africa. Researchers believe, however, that the number of reported cases is vastly lower than the actual number of cases. Officials at the World Health Organization estimate that there are at least 200,000 new cases per year, including 30,000 deaths, with 90% of cases occurring in Africa.

Epidemics of yellow fever were widespread from the seventeenth century until the early twentieth century. These epidemics were tied to the spread of the *A. aegypti* mosquito, as a result of an increase in shipping and commerce. The first recorded epidemic of what was thought to be yellow fever occurred in the Yucatán Peninsula, in what is now Mexico, in the mid-seventeenth century. For the next 300 years, yellow fever was the most important epidemic disease in the New World. Though it is no longer a problem in the United States, yellow fever once caused summer epidemics that ranged as far north as Boston, Massachusetts, from the seventeenth through the nineteenth centuries.

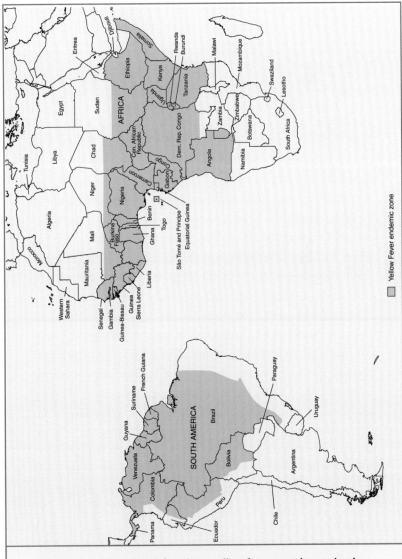

Figure 8.1 Map of regions where yellow fever remains endemic. Portions of South America and Africa where outbreaks of the virus are common are shaded in blue. (Centers for Disease Control and Prevention)

Little was known about the virus until the early 1900s, when a physician named Walter Reed showed that yellow fever was caused by a "filterable agent" (a virus) that was transmitted by the *A. aegypti* mosquito. Following this revelation, prevention of yellow fever focused on control of the mosquito population. These measures resulted in a dramatic decrease in epidemics. In addition, a vaccine is available for yellow fever, further aiding in the reduction of the frequency of epidemics.

The incubation period for this illness is roughly three to six days. Symptoms, including fever, headache, nausea, vomiting, and **bradycardia** (slow heartbeat), come on suddenly. In many cases, yellow fever is a biphasic (having two phases) illness. The patient becomes ill, the illness seems to resolve somewhat, and then the patient becomes ill again. Jaundice, a yellowing of the skin and eyes due to the buildup of a protein called bilirubin, is often present in the second phase of the disease and might be present in the initial phase. This hallmark symptom gives the illness its name. The fatality rate ranges between 20% and 50%.

In some parts of the world, yellow fever has undergone a resurgence in recent years. Outbreaks have occurred in Nigeria, Liberia, Cameroon, Kenya, and the Ivory Coast in Africa, as well as Peru, Ecuador, Venezuela, Bolivia, and Brazil in South America. Outbreaks have generally been confined to rural areas, although in Nigeria, Ivory Coast, and Bolivia the disease occurred in urban areas. Travelers to these countries are in danger of infection. Scientists have documented six cases of fatal yellow fever in travelers in Africa and the Americas since 1990. Yellow fever is the only hemorrhagic fever for which there is an effective vaccine. The vaccine is in limited supply, however, and is not used routinely for prevention in areas where yellow fever is endemic.

DENGUE

Dengue virus is related to the yellow fever virus. Both viruses are flaviviruses transmitted by mosquitoes. Whereas yellow fever circulates in the rain forests of Africa and the Amazon basin in South America, dengue viruses are found in similar areas

Figure 8.2 The *Aedes aegypti* mosquito is able to transmit both the yellow fever and dengue viruses. Both diseases have been controlled in some countries (including the United States) through aggressive mosquito elimination programs; however, they still remain a large problem in many areas of the world. (Centers for Disease Control and Prevention)

of Asia and West Africa. Both dengue and yellow fever can be transmitted by the *Aedes aegypti* mosquito (Figure 8.2).

Similar to yellow fever, dengue used to be prevalent in the Americas. Epidemics that were most likely caused by the dengue virus occurred as early as 1635 in the West Indies, with another large outbreak in 1699 in Central America. Epidemics were also common in the United States into the 1930s. A large outbreak occurred in Philadelphia, Pennsylvania, in 1790. The last large outbreak in the United States ended in 1945 in New Orleans, Louisiana. The same programs used to control the mosquito population in yellow fever epidemics also aided in the elimination of dengue.

Both dengue and yellow fever infection in humans cause a range of disease, from a very mild illness to severe hemorrhagic disease. The latter is an uncommon manifestation of dengue virus infection. Approximately 500,000 cases of dengue hemorrhagic fever occur each year, out of a total of 50–100 million dengue infections; thus, only around 1 in 100 infections with dengue virus results in dengue hemorrhagic fever. A more common symptom of dengue virus infection is severe back pain—*dengue* means "break-back." The fatality rate for this virus is about 5%, but rates as high as 40% have been documented in some epidemics.

Over the last 30 years, there has been a resurgence in cases of dengue virus infection in all tropical parts of the world, including cases in Florida in 2009–2010.

HANTAVIRUS

Hantaviruses are members of the *Bunyaviridae* family carried by rodents. These viruses can be found in the Americas, Asia, and Europe. Hantaviruses cause two serious diseases in humans: hantavirus pulmonary syndrome, and hantavirus hemorrhagic fever with renal syndrome (HFRS). The latter disease came to the attention of American doctors largely as a result of the Korean War (1950–1953). Approximately 3,000 soldiers contracted this disease. Mortality was approximately 7%. Four recognized species of hantavirus cause this disease: Dobrava, Hantaan, Puumala, and Seoul viruses. Similar to the different species of Ebola viruses, these species differ in their virulence potential. Hantaan and Dobrava generally cause the most severe disease. Seoul virus causes moderately severe disease, while Puumala virus generally causes mild HFRS. Several hantaviruses have been found in the United States. Most of these, however, are not known to cause HFRS. Seoul virus is the only HFRS-causing virus that has a worldwide distribution.

Rodents act as reservoirs for the hantaviruses. Virus is excreted in their urine. When the urine dries, the virus can be aerosolized and inadvertently inhaled by humans, causing disease. Virus can also be ingested when rodent **excreta** (fecal matter or urine) are present on food, or via direct contact with this material. There are currently vaccines available against

HPS IN THE UNITED STATES

Although the Seoul virus and other hantatviruses can cause hemorrhagic fever, another species of hantavirus has become more famous in the United States. In early May 1993, a small community in New Mexico was shocked and saddened by the deaths of two young people within five days of each other. The victims were only 19 and 21 years old, respectively, and were living in the same household. The illness came on suddenly in both of them, with fever, headache, cough, and a general feeling of sickness. These symptoms rapidly led to pneumonia and respiratory failure. By May 17, a total of five people had died from this strange disease. Scientists conducted a study to look for a common exposure. Physicians found that similar cases had been diagnosed in Arizona, Utah, and Colorado, as well as several others in New Mexico. After an extensive investigation, the scientific investigators determined that the cause of disease was a rodent-borne hantavirus that had not been described previously. Originally referred to as the "Four Corners Virus" due to the location of the earliest known cases, it was finally given the name *"Sin Nombre Virus"*—the virus without a name. Since this time, the virus has been found retrospectively in cases of people who died from similar symptoms, showing that it had been circulating in the country and causing disease without being recognized. This illustrates the need for constant surveillance of pathogens, both old and new.

some strains of hantavirus (Hantaan and Seoul). Ribavirin is useful as a treatment if given early enough during infection and at sufficiently high doses.

LASSA

Lassa virus is an arenavirus that causes Lassa fever. Similar to hantavirus, transmission occurs as a result of the inhalation of aerosols of rodent urine or feces, through ingestion of food contaminated with rodent droppings, or through direct contact with broken skin or mucous membranes of an infected person. Person-to-person transmission is possible, generally as a result of direct contact with infected bodily fluids. Airborne transmission is also thought to be possible, but it appears to be rare. Unlike most of the other hemorrhagic fevers, Lassa fever is gradual in onset, and the illness tends to be more severe during pregnancy. Particularly in the third trimester of pregnancy, fatality from Lassa disease is quite high for the mother, and spontaneous abortion of the fetus often results. Like Ebola, the virus seems to be maintained in the body during an extended period of convalescence. The virus has been detected in semen up to three months after acute infection, and in urine a month after disease onset. The overall fatality rate is less than 2%, but ranges between 15% and 20% for untreated cases. Approximately 5,000 deaths occur as a result of Lassa fever every year.

RIFT VALLEY

Like Ebola, Rift Valley fever is named after the geographic area where it was first detected, Kenya's Rift Valley. Rift Valley fever is a **zoonosis** (a disease that is transmitted between human and animal species), and is caused by a virus in the family *Bunyaviridae*. This virus causes not only death of the adult animal, but is also a major cause of spontaneous abortion in livestock. A major epidemic in 1997–1998 in East Africa killed large numbers of livestock. Human cases during this outbreak were estimated to number around 89,000. An outbreak that occurred in 2000 marked the first time the disease was found outside of Africa, infecting both livestock and humans in Saudi Arabia and Yemen. The spread of this disease is ominous, as there is little to stop this virus from entering new areas. Though the Rift Valley fever virus is typically spread by direct contact with infected animals or their products, it can also be transmitted by the bite of an infected mosquito. Indeed, outbreaks of Rift Valley fever often occur in years when there are heavy rains and localized flooding, leading to an increase in the mosquito population. The disease is not thought to be transmitted from person to person via everyday contact. Infections in a laboratory setting are also possible. In humans, only a small percentage of infections proceed to hemorrhage, and fatality occurs in about 1% of patients. Symptoms of this disease are similar to those found in the other hemorrhagic fevers. Early symptoms generally include headache, fever, and sore throat. A skin rash may be present, and Rift Valley fever may also cause jaundice, as seen with yellow fever. Other possible outcomes include vision loss, which occurs in 1% to 10% of patients, and **encephalitis** (inflammation of the brain). Some people are infected but do not show any symptoms of disease. Ribavirin may be used to treat this virus. There is no vaccine available to prevent Rift Valley fever.

SUMMARY

The viruses that cause hemorrhagic fever vary in prevalence and lethality. Ebola and Marburg are two of the most deadly, but at the same time, are the rarest in incidence. Most of these viral illnesses occur in Africa and South America, so scientists in the United States have not made research a high priority. As the Reston, Virginia, Ebola outbreak has shown, however, no one can really be "safe" from these viral illnesses. As humans clear more forested areas and encroach on new habitats, new viruses are emerging from the environment as we are exposed with greater frequency to animals and insects that humans previously encountered only rarely. This increased exposure to new organisms also means an increased likelihood of exposure to the pathogens they carry—some of which are likely to be highly virulent for humans and our domestic animals. Basic research into viruses that may not appear to be an immediate threat may not seem to be necessary. Increasing our understanding of these pathogens, however, could have unexpected benefits.

Notes

Chapter 1

1. World Health Organization, "Marburg Haemorrhagic Fever: Fact Sheet," March 31, 2005, http://www.who.int/csr/disease/marburg/factsheet/en/ (accessed May 19, 2010); W. Slenczka and H. D. Klenk, "Forty Years of Marburg Virus," *Journal of Infectious Diseases* 196, Suppl. 2 (November 15, 2007): S131–5.

Chapter 2

1. D. G. Bausch et al., "Risk Factors for Marburg Hemorrhagic Fever, Democratic Republic of the Congo," *Emerging Infectious Diseases 9* (2003): 1531–1537; B. Beer and R. Kurth, "Characteristics of Filoviridae: Marburg and Ebola Viruses," *Naturwissenschaften*, 86 (1999): 8–17; A. Burton, "Marburg Miner Mystery," *The Lancet Infectious Diseases 4* (2004): R. Preston, *The Hot Zone* (New York: Random House, 1994); CIDRAP News, "Angola Declares Worst Marburg Outbreak Over," November 10, 2005, http://www.cidrap.umn.edu/cidrap/content/bt/vhf/news/nov1005marburg.html (accessed May 19, 2010); World Health Organization, "Marburg Virus in Uganda," August 3, 2007, http://www.who.int/csr/don/2007_08_03/en/index.html (accessed May 19, 2010); Robert Roos, "Marburg Fever Case Reported in Netherlands," CIDRAP News, July 10, 2008, http://www.cidrap.umn.edu/cidrap/content/bt/vhf/news/jul1008marburg.html (accessed May 19, 2010).

2. D. G. Bausch et al., "Risk Factors for Marburg Hemorrhagic Fever, Democratic Republic of the Congo," *Emerging Infectious Diseases* Dec. 2003, http://www.cdc.gov/ncidod/EID/vol9no12/03-0355.htm (accessed May 19, 2010).

Chapter 3

1. Centers for Disease Control and Prevention, "Known Cases and Outbreaks of Ebola Hemorrhagic Fever, in Chronological Order," http://www.cdc.gov/ncidod/dvrd/spb/mnpages/dispages/ebola/ebolatable.htm (updated April 12, 2010); J. S. Towner et al., "Newly Discovered Ebola Virus Associated with Hemorrhagic Fever Outbreak in Uganda," *PLoS Pathogens* 4, no. 11 (Nov. 2008): e1000212, http://www.plospathogens.org/article/info:doi/10.1371/journal.ppat.1000212 (accessed May 19, 2010); R. W. Barrette, "Discovery of Swine as a Host for the Reston Ebolavirus," *Science* 325, no. 5937 (July 10, 2009): 204–6.

Chapter 5

1. N. Fujita et al., "Imported Case of Marburg Hemorrhagic Fever — Colorado, 2008," *Morbidity and Mortality Weekly Reports* 58, no. 49 (December 18, 2009): 1377-1381, http://www.cdc.gov/mmwr/preview/mmwrhtml/mm5849a2.htm (accessed May 18, 2010).

2. E. M. Leroy et al., "Fruit Bats as Reservoirs of Ebola Virus," *Nature* 438 (December 1, 2005): 575–6; J. S. Towner et al., "Marburg Virus Infection Detected in a Common African Bat," *PLoS One* 2, no. 1 (August 22, 2007): e764; E. M. Leroy et al., "Human Ebola Outbreak Resulting from Direct Exposure to Fruit Bats in Luebo, Democratic Republic of Congo, 2007," *Vector Borne Zoonotic Diseases* 9 (December 2009): 723–8.

Chapter 7

1. J. S. Towner et al., "Newly Discovered Ebola Virus Associated with Hemorrhagic Fever Outbreak in Uganda." *PLoS Pathogens* 4, no. 11 (November 2008): e1000212.

adenovirus—Any DNA-containing viruses shaped like a 20-sided polyhedron that cause conjunctivitis and upper respiratory tract infections and even the common cold in humans.

amino acids—The building blocks of proteins.

anorexia—Lack of appetite or unwillingness to eat.

antibodies—Proteins present in the blood that recognize and bind to specific portions of foreign proteins, targeting them for clearance by other cells of the immune system.

antigens—Portions of a pathogen's proteins that are targets of the host immune system.

antivirals—Drugs that block the replication of viruses.

arthropods—Invertebrate animals that include insects, crustaceans, and spiders.

asymptomatic—Without no symptoms.

barrier nursing procedures—The act of placing a physical barrier between oneself and a pathogenic microbe while caring for patients. These barriers include wearing gloves, masks, and gowns over the body. Regular hand-washing is also implemented with this practice.

B cells—Cells of the host immune system that produce antibodies.

biosafety level 4 (BSL-4)—Involving an agent that is highly lethal and has no known cure or vaccine. These pathogens can only be worked on in a specially equipped laboratory.

booster—Shots of vaccine given subsequent to the first dose in an effort to increase the effectiveness of the host immune response.

bradycardia—Slow heartbeat.

bunyavirus—A group of enveloped, single-stranded RNA viruses.

chemokines—A subset of cytokines that play a role in the movement and activation of other cells of the immune system.

cleave—In biochemistry, using one protein to cut another.

conjugate—In molecular biology, the process of linking one protein to another, generally for diagnostic purposes.

control group—A group that does not receive treatment in order to determine if a particular treatment is effective. The control group is compared with the treated group to measure a difference in outcome.

convalescence—The process of recovery from infection.

cytokines—Proteins made by cells that affect the behavior of other groups of cells in the immune system, allowing the body to fight infectious disease.

cytotoxicity—Ability to cause toxic damage to infected cells.

disseminated intravascular coagulation (DIC)—The phenomenon in which blood clots within the capillaries, which can lead to bleeding throughout the body. This is a hallmark of Ebola virus infection.

ecology—The study of an organism's natural environment and its interaction with both this environment and with other organisms within.

electron microscopy—The process of using electrons rather than visible light to magnify an image.

ELISA (Enzyme-linked immunosorbant assay)—A diagnostic test that looks for the presence of antibodies to a particular pathogen in the serum of a subject.

emerging pathogens—Pathogens that have been recently discovered as a cause of disease in humans or animals.

encephalitis—Inflammation of the brain.

endemic—Occurring in an area on a regular basis.

epidemiologist—A scientist who studies the patterns of diseases.

epithelium—The layer of tissue covering the internal and external surfaces of the body.

euthanize—The act or practice of killing or permitting the death of individuals suffering from terminal illness or incurable conditions in a relatively painless way.

excreta—A collective term for feces and urine.

fatality rate—Calculated by looking at the number of deaths divided by the number of infected individuals, thus it shows how many of the infected individuals are killed by the disease. Ebola's fatality rate is higher than almost any other disease.

filoviridae—A family of thread-like viruses that includes both the Ebola and Marburg viruses.

fluorescein—A protein used in diagnostics. Under fluorescent light, this proteins emits a fluorescent color.

gene—A stretch of DNA that encodes a particular protein.

genetic diversity—The amount of variation at the DNA level within a species.

genome—All of an organism's genetic material.

guano—Excrement of bats.

hemorrhage—Severe bleeding.

hemorrhagic—Causing hemorrhage.

HEPA filters—Filters with very tiny pores, too small for even viral particles to pass through.

histamines—A protein produced by cells of the body's immune system that causes dilution of blood vessels; also involved in allergic reactions.

immune response—The body's defense against pathogens.

immunoglobulins—See **antibodies**.

incubation period—The time between exposure to a pathogen and the development of symptoms of disease.

index case—The first person in an outbreak known to be infected.

indirect fluorescence assay (IFA)—A serological test using fluorescein, which shows if a subject has the presence of antibodies to a particular pathogen.

interferon—A type of cytokine that can induce cells to resist viral replication.

jaundice—A yellowing of the skin and eyes due to the buildup of bilirubin, a byproduct of the breakdown of red blood cells, or evidence of liver dysfunction.

killed vaccine—A vaccine in which the pathogen is killed prior to injection, and therefore is unable to replicate within the body.

live attenuated vaccine—A vaccine in which the pathogen is able to replicate in the body, but causes no symptoms of disease.

macaque—A type of monkey, commonly used for research purposes.

morbidity—A measure of illness in the population due to a specific disease.

morphology—The shape or appearance of an object.

mortality rate—Number of deaths due to a specific disease.

naturally acquired infections—Infections acquired in nature rather than in a laboratory setting.

necropsy—An examination made after death.

nosocomial—Occurring primarily in a hospital.

pathogenesis—Origin and development of disease.

PCR (polymerase chain reaction)—A process of amplification of a particular portion of nucleic acid, often a gene. This can be used for diagnosis of infection and analysis of the infecting pathogen.

peridomestic—Referring to wild animals that are commonly found around human settlements; for example, the common house mouse.

phagocytes—Cells of the host immune system that engulf and destroy foreign material, including pathogens.

phylogenetic tree—A visual description of the genetic diversity and ancestry in a population of organisms.

poaching—Illegal hunting.

polymerase—An enzyme that catalyzes the polymerization of nucleotides.

primatologists—Scientists who study primates.

primer—A small DNA fragment that is complementary to a sequence on a DNA template. Binding of primers to the template allows DNA polymerase to create a complementary strand of DNA during the polymerase chain reaction.

reservoir—The habitat of a pathogen in nature. This often refers to an animal or insect (a reservoir host), but might also refer to an environment (such as a body of water).

ring vaccination—A vaccination protocol in which contacts of a case are vaccinated first, followed by contacts of these vaccinated individuals, so that "rings" of protection are made around a known case of disease.

RNAses—Commonly found proteins that break down and destroy RNA.

RNA virus—A virus whose geneic material consists of ribonucleic acid, or RNA.

savannah—Flat grassland in tropical or subtropical regions.

secondary case—Any infected patient who contracted disease as a result of the index (or primary) case.

secreted—Released from cells.

sensitivity—The ability of a procedure to correctly identify positive samples from all the samples submitted for testing from infected subjects.

serological evidence—Serum antibody responses documenting current or past infection with an organism.

seroprevalence—The amount of disease in a population, as measured via studies of antibodies to an organism present in the serum of a population.

serum—The liquid (acellular) portion of the blood, which contains antibodies.

shock—A medical condition characterized by a severe drop in blood pressure.

simian hemorrhagic fever (SHF)—A virus occurring in monkeys that causes symptoms similar to Ebola virus. SHF is not harmful to humans.

specificity—The ability of a test to correctly identify negative samples from all samples submitted from patients without infection.

strain—Organisms that share the same genetic makeup; clones.

subclinical—See **asymptomatic**.

substrate—The substance on which an enzyme acts.

subtype—In microbiology, a group within a species; slightly different variants of the virus.

T cell—A type of cell in the body's immune system that is generally most important in defense against viruses and other intracellular pathogens.

template—A DNA sequence that serves as a pattern for the synthesis of a complementary strand.

tertiary case—Any infected patient who contracted the disease as a result of exposure to a secondary case.

thermophile—An organism that lives in very hot environments; "heat-loving."

transfused—Given blood intravenously.

transovarially—Transmitted from the mother to an offspring directly via the egg (ovum).

USAMRIID—U.S. Army Medical Research Institute of Infectious Diseases. This institute is located at Fort Detrick, Maryland. Research is carried out there on diseases with military implications, including defensive measures against biological warfare.

vaccine—Suspensions of either dead or weakened pathogen, or products produced by the pathogen, designed to cause immunity to the pathogen in the host.

vectors—Agents (usually insects) that transmit a pathogen from one host to another.

viral envelope—The outermost portion of a virus.

viremia—The presence of virus in the blood.

virulence—The severity of clinical illness resulting from infection.

zoonosis—A disease that is transmitted between animal species and humans.

Bibliography

Arthur, R. R. "Ebola in Africa: Discoveries in the Past Decade." *Eurosurveillance* 7 (2002): 33–36.

Baron, R. C., et al. "Ebola Virus Disease in Southern Sudan: Hospital Dissemination and Intrafamilial Spread." *Bulletin of the World Health Organization* 61 (1983): 997–103.

Bausch, D. G., et al. "Risk Factors for Marburg Hemorrhagic Fever, Democratic Republic of the Congo." *Emerging Infectious Diseases* 9 (2003): 1531–1537.

Beer B., and R. Kurth. "Characteristics of Filoviridae: Marburg and Ebola Viruses." *Naturwissenschaften* 86 (1999): 8–17.

Boehman, Y., S. Enterlein, A. Randolf, and E. Muhlberger. "A Reconstituted Replication and Transcription System for Ebola Virus Reston and Comparison with Ebola Virus Zaire." *Virology* 332 (2005):406–417.

Borio, L., et al. "Hemorrhagic Fever Viruses as Biological Weapons." *Journal of the American Medical Association* 287 (2002): 2391–2405.

Bouree, P. and J. F. Bergmann. "Ebola Virus Infection in Man: a Serological and Epidemiological Survey in the Cameroons." *American Journal of Tropical Medicine and Hygiene* 32 (1983): 1465–1466.

Breman, J. G., G. van der Groen, D. L. Heymann, F. Meier, K. M. Johnson, C. B. Robbins, K. Ruti, M. V. Szczeniowski, K. Webb, et al. "A Search for Ebola Virus in Animals in the Democratic Republic of the Congo and Cameroon: Ecologic, Virologic, and Serologic Surveys, 1979–80." *Journal of Infectious Diseases* 179, S1(1999): S139–147.

Burton, A. "Marburg Miner Mystery." *The Lancet Infections Disease* 4 (2004).

Burton, P. "Fighting the Ebola Virus." *Nature* 408 (2000): 527–528.

Busico, K. M., T. G. Ksiazek, K. L. Marshall, et al. "Prevalence of IgG Antibodies to Ebola Virus in Individuals During an Ebola Outbreak, Democratic Republic of the Congo 1995." *Journal of Infectious Diseases* 179 (1999): S102–107.

Centers for Disease Control and Prevention. "Brief Report: Outbreak of Marburg Virus Hemorrhagic Fever—Angola, October 1, 2004–March 29, 2005." *Morbidity and Mortality Weekly Report* 54 (2005): 1–2.

———."Management of Patients with Suspected Viral Hemorrhagic Fever." *Morbidity and Mortality Weekly Report* 37S3 (1998): 1–16.

———."Outbreak of Acute Illness—Southwestern United States, 1993." *Morbidity and Mortality Weekly Report* 42 (1993): 421–424.

Clement, J. P. "Hantavirus." *Antiviral Reseach* 57 (2003): 121–127.

Colebunders R., H. Sleurs, P. Pirard, M. Borchert, M. Libande, J. P. Mustin, A. Tshomba, L. Kinuani, L. A. Olinda, F. Tshioko, and J. J. Muyembe-Tamfum. "Organisation of Health Care During an Outbreak of Marburg Haemorrhagic Fever in the Democratic Republic of Congo, 1999." *Journal of Infection* 48 (2004): 347–353.

Dove, A. "Ebola Vaccine Gets Corporate Backer." *Nature Medicine* 8 (2002): 645–646.

Formentry, P., C. Boesch, F. Dind, F. Donati, B. LeGeunno, C. Steiner, F. Walker, and M. Wyers. "Ebola Virus Outbreak Among Wild Chimpanzees Living in a Rain Forest of Côte d'Ivoire." *Journal of Infectious Diseases* 179,S1(1999): S120–126.

Formentry, P., C. Hatz, B. LeGuenno, P. Rogenmoser, A. Stoll, and A. Widmer. "Human Infection Due to Ebola Virus, Subtype Côte d'Ivoire: Clinical and Biologic Presentation." *Journal of Infectious Diseases* 179, Suppl 1(1999): S48–53.

Garrett, L. *The Coming Plague.* New York: Penguin Books, 1994.

Georges, A-J., et al. "Ebola Hemorrhagic Fever Outbreaks in Gabon, 1994–1997: Epidemiologic and Health Control Issues." *Journal of Infectious Diseases* 179, Suppl 1 (1999): S65–75.

Georges-Corbot, M-C., et al. "Isolation and Phylogenetic Characterization of Ebola Viruses Causing Different Outbreaks in Gabon." *Emerging Infectious Diseases* 3 (1997): 59–62.

Gonzalez, J. P., E. D. Johnson, R. Josse, et al. "Antibody Prevalence Against Haemorrhagic Fever Viruses in Random Representative Central African Populations." *Research in Virology* 140 (1989): 319–331.

Gonzalez, J. P., J. M. Morvan, E. Nakoune, W. Slenczka, and P. Vidal. "Ebola and Marburg Virus Antibody Prevalence in Selected Populations of the Central African Republic." *Microbes and Infection* 2 (2000): 39–44.

Gubler, D. J. "The Changing Epidemiology of Yellow Fever and Dengue, 1990–2003: Full Circle?" *Comparative Immunology, Microbiology, and Infectious Diseases* 27 (2004): 319–330.

Hart, M. K. "Vaccine Research Efforts for Filoviruses." *International Journal for Parasitology* 33 (2003): 583–595.

Isaäcson, M. "Viral Hemorrhagic Fever Hazards for Travelers in Africa." *Clinical Infectious Diseases* 33 (2001): 1707–1712.

Jahrling P. B., et al. "Evaluation of Immune Globulin and Recombinant Interferon-?2b for Treatment of Experimental Ebola Virus Infections." *Journal of Infectious Diseases* 179, Suppl. 1(1999): S224–234.

Jezek, Z., D. L. Heymann, J. B. McCormick, J. J. Muyembe-Tamfum, and M. Y. Szczeniowski. "Ebola Between Outbreaks: Intensified Ebola Hemorrhagic Fever Surveillance in the Democratic Republic of the Congo, 1981–85." *Journal of Infectious Diseases* 179,S1 (1999): S60–64.

Khan A. S., et al. "The Reemergence of Ebola Hemorrhagic Fever, Democratic Republic of the Congo, 1995." *Journal of Infectious Diseases* 179, Suppl. 1 (1999): S76–86.

Ksiazek, T. G., C. J. Peters, P. R. Jahrling, P. E. Rollins, and C. P. West. "ELISA for the Detection of Antibodies to Ebola Viruses." *Journal of Infectious Diseases* 179, Suppl. 1 (1999): S192–198.

Lednicky, J. A. "Hantaviruses: A Short Review." *Archives of Pathology and Laboratory Medicine* 127 (2003): 30–36.

Leirs, H., D. Akaibe, J. E. Childs, J. W. Krebs, T. G. Ksiazek, G. Ludwig, J. N. Mills, C. J. Peters, and N. Woollen. "Search for the Ebola Virus Reservoir in Kikwit, Democratic Republic of the Congo: Reflections on a Vertebrate Collection." *Journal of Infectious Diseases* 179, Suppl. 1 (1999): S155–163.

Leroy, E. M., P. Rouquet, P. Formentry, S. Souquiere, A. Kilbourne, J-M. Froment, M. Bermejo, S. Smit, W. Karesh, R. Swanepoel, S. R. Zaki, and P. E. Rollin. "Multiple Ebola Virus Transmission Events and Rapid Decline of Central African Wildlife." *Science* 303 (2004): 387–390.

Lovegreen, S. "Ebola Outbreak Wracks Uganda." October 19, 2000. Available online at *www.msnbc.com*.

Lundsgaard, T. "Filovirus-like Particles Detected in the Leafhopper *Psammotettix alienus*." *Virus Research* 48(1997): 35–40.

McCormick, J. B. "Ebola Virus Ecology." *Journal of Infectious Diseases* 190 (2004): 1893–1894.

Miller, R. K. "Update: Filovirus Infections Among Persons with Occupational Exposure to Nonhuman Primates." *Morbidity and Mortality Weekly Report* 39 (1990): 266–267.

Miranda, M. E., et al. "Epidemiology of Ebola (Subtype Reston) Virus in the Philippines, 1996." *Journal of Infectious Diseases* 179, Suppl1 (1999): S115–119.

Monath, T. P. "Ecology of Marburg and Ebola Viruses: Speculations and Directions for Future Research." *Journal of Infectious Diseases* 179, Suppl. 1 (1999): S127–138.

Mupapa, K. et al. "Treatment of Ebola Hemorrhagic Fever with Blood Transfusions from Convalescent Patients." *Journal of Infectious Diseases* 179, Suppl. 1 (1999): S18–23.

Mutebi, J-P. and A. D. T. Barrett. "The Epidemiology of Yellow Fever in Africa." *Microbes and Infection* 4 (2002): 1459–1468.

Mwanatambwe, M., N. Yamada, S. Aria, M. Shimizu-Suganuma, K. Shichinohe, and G. Asano. "Ebola Hemorrhagic Fever (EHF): Mechanism of Transmission and Pathogenicity." *Journal of Nippon Medical School* 68 (2001): 370–375.

Osterholm, M. T., and J. Schwartz. *Living Terrors*. New York: Delacorte Press, 2000.

Peters C. J., and J. W. LeDuc. "An Introduction to Ebola: the Virus and the Disease." *Journal of Infectious Diseases* 179, Suppl. 1 (1999): ix–xvi.

Peterson, A. T., D. S. Carroll, J. N. Mills, and K. M. Johnson. "Potential Mammalian Filovirus Reservoirs." *Emerging Infectious Diseases* 10 (2004): 2073–2081.

Peterson A. T., J. T. Bauer, and J. N. Mills. "Ecologic and Geographic Distribution of Filovirus Disease." *Emerging Infectious Diseases* 10 (2004): 40–47.

Preston, R. *The Hot Zone*. New York: Random House, 1994.

Rollin, P. E., et al. "Ebola (Subtype Reston) Virus among Quarantined Nonhuman Primates Recently Imported from the Philippines to the United States." *Journal of Infectious Diseases* 179, Suppl. (1999): S108–114.

Sanchez, A., T. G. Ksiazek, P. E. Rollin, M. E. G. Miranda, S. G. Trappier, A. S. Khan, C. J. Peters, and S. T. Nichol. "Detection and Molecular Characterization of Ebola Viruses Causing Disease in Human and Nonhuman Primates." *Journal of Infectious Diseases* 179, Suppl. 1 (1999): S164–169.

Sullivan, N. J., T. W. Geisbert, J. B. Geisbert, L. Xu, Z. Yang, M. Roederer, R. A. Koup, P. B. Jahrling, and G. J. Nabel. "Accelerated Vaccination for Ebola Virus Haemorrhagic Fever in Non-human Primates." *Nature* 424 (2003): 681–684.

Swanepoel, R., P. A. Leman, F. J. Burt, N. J. Zachariades, L. E. Braack, T. G. Ksiazek, P. E. Rollin, S. R. Zaki, and C. J. Peters. "Experimental Inoculation of Plants and Animals with Ebola Virus." *Emerging Infectious Diseases* 2 (1996): 321–325.

Takada, A., et al. "Infectivity-enhancing Antibodies to Ebola Virus Glyco-protein." *Journal of Virology* 75 (2001): 2324–2330.

Takada, A., and Y. Kawaoka. "The Pathogenesis of Ebola Hemorrhagic Fever." *Trends in Microbiology* 9 (2001): 506–511.

Turell, M. J., D. S. Bressler, and C. A. Rossi. "Short Report: Lack of Virus Replication in Arthropods After Intrathoracic Inoculation of Ebola Reston Virus." *American Journal of Tropical Medicine and Hygiene* 55 (1996): 89–90.

Vogel, G. "Can Great Apes Be Saved from Ebola?" *Science* 300 (2003): 1645.

Wilson, J. A., M. Bray, R. Bakken, and M. K. Hart. "Vaccine Potential of Ebola Virus VP24, VP30, VP35, and VP40 Proteins." *Virology* 286 (2001): 384–390.

Zaki, S. R., S. Wun-Ju, P. W. Greer, C. S. Goldsmith, et al. "A Novel Immunohis-tochemical Assay for the Detection of Ebola Virus in Skin: Implications for Diagnosis, Spread, and Surveillance of Ebola Hemorrhagic Fever." *Journal of Infectious Diseases* 179, Suppl. 1 (1999): S36–47.

Further Resources

Books

Close, W. *Ebola*. New York: Ivy Books, 1995.

Garrett, L. *The Coming Plague*. New York: Penguin Books, 1994.

McCormick, J. B. *Level 4: Virus Hunters of the CDC*. New York: Barnes and Noble Books, 1996.

Morse, S. S., ed. *Emerging Viruses*. New York: Oxford University Press, 1993.

Preston, R. *The Hot Zone*. New York: Random House, 1994.

Web Sites

Centers for Disease Control and Prevention (CDC):
http://www.cdc.gov

CDC Viral Hemorrhagic Fevers page:
http://www.cdc.gov/ncidod/diseases/virlfvr/virlfvr.htm

Emerging Infectious Diseases journal:
http://www.cdc.gov/ncidod/eid/

National Institutes of Health:
http://www.nih.gov/

World Health Organization (WHO), Ebola site:
http://www.who.int/csr/disease/ebola/en/

Index

Page numbers in *italics* indicate illustrations. Page numbers followed by *t* indicate charts or tables.

adenovirus, 73, 86
Aedes aegypti, 76, 78, *79*
Africa
  Ebola virus, *14,* 17–28, *24, 27t*
  filovirus-infected bats, 54–56
  Marburg virus, 12, *14,* 15
  Rift Valley fever, 82
  seroprevalence, 46, 52, 56–57
  yellow fever, 76, *77,* 78
African green monkeys, 9
amino acids, 37, 86
Angola, 12–14, *14*
anorexia, 36, 86
antibodies, 86
  B cells, 70
  detection methods, 58–63
  human, 16, 29, 39, 56
  indirect fluorescence assay, *59, 60*
  nonhuman primate, 52
  treatment methods, 63–65
antigens, 58, 60, 73, 86
antivirals, 63, 86
arthropods, 46–47, 51, 86
Asia, 46
asymptomatic infections, 54, 86
Aum Shinrikyo, 69
avian influenza (H5N1), 6

barrier nursing procedures, 13, 41, 67, 86
bats, 44–45, 49
  Egyptian fruit bat, *50*
  filovirus reservoir, 12
  guano, 44, 54, 88
  Marburg virus, 54, 56
  Sudan outbreak, 19
B cells, 70, 86
biological terrorism, 68–69
biosafety level 1 (BSL-1) laboratories, 30

biosafety level 2 (BSL-2) laboratories, 30
biosafety level 3 (BSL-3) laboratories, 30–31
biosafety level 4 (BSL-4) laboratories, 31, *32,* 61, 86
biosafety levels (generally), 30–31
booster, 73, 86
Bovine Spongiform Encephalopathy (BSE), 6
bradycardia, 78, 86
BSE (Bovine Spongiform Encephalopathy), 6
BSL. *See* biosafety level *entries*
Bunyaviridae, 80, 82
bunyavirus, 75, 86

Cameroon, 52
CCHF (Crimean-Congo hemorraghic fever virus), 75–76
Centers for Disease Control and Prevention (CDC), 18
Cercopithecus aethiops, 9
chemokines, 36, 86
chimpanzees, 20–22, 52, 53, *55. See also* nonhuman primates
cleaving, 61, 86
clinical symptoms, 35–36, 68
Colobus badius, 53
The Coming Plague (Laurie Garrett), 34
communicable diseases, 6
conjugation, 58, 86
control groups, 64, 65, 86
convalescence, 42, 87
Cote d'Ivoire. *See* Ivory Coast
Creutzfeldt-Jakob disease (vCJD), 6
Crimean-Congo hemorraghic fever virus (CCHF), 75–76
Crucell, 74
cytokines, 36, 87
cytotoxicity, 37, 87

deaths. *See* fatality rates; mortality rates
Democratic Republic of the Congo

(DRC), *14*
  1976 Ebola outbreak, 9–10, 17, 47,
    49
  1995 Ebola outbreak, 22, 64–65
  bunyavirus, 75
  Ebola ecology, 51
  Ebola Zaire, 26, 42
  fruit bat migration, 56
  Marburg virus, 12, 13, 15
dengue, 46, 78–80, *79*
deoxyribonucleic acid (DNA), 64
detection of filoviruses, 58–63
  metagenomics, 62–63
  PCR-based methods, 61–62
  tests, 58–61
disseminated intravascular coagulation
  (DIC), 36, 87
Doctors without Borders, 13
DRC. *See* Democratic Republic of the
  Congo

Ebola Bundibugyo (EBO-B), 26, 45
Ebola Côte d'Ivoire (EBO-IC), 21, 45
Ebola Reston (EBO-R), 45
  cytotoxicity, 38–39
  Hazelton Research laboratory,
    28–30
  media publicity, 34
  Philippines, 26, 33, 46
  transmission, 67–68
Ebola Sudan (EBO-S), 20, 23, 45, 49
Ebola virus, 17–34. *See also specific*
    Ebola subtypes
  2000-2001 outbreak, *24, 27t*
  in Africa. *See* Africa; *specific*
    African countries
  antibody test, *59*
  biological weapon, 68–69
  incubation period, 35–36, 67
  media publicity, 34
  morphology, *9*
  nonhuman primates. *See* nonhu-
    man primates
  protective suits, *71*

"Red Death," 40–41
reservoirs. *See* reservoirs
  schematic drawing, *38*
  subtypes of, 35, 44–46
  transmission. *See* transmission
  treatment, 63–65
  in United States, 28–34, 66
Ebola Zaire (EBO-Z), 45
  1976 outbreak, 20
  2001-2002 outbreak, 25
  biological weapon, 68
  cytotoxicity, 38
  Democratic Republic of Congo,
    23, 26
  ecology, 49
  immune response, 39
  subtypes, 35
  transmission, 42
ecology of filoviruses, 43–57, 87
  epidemiology, 44–48
  infection in humans, 56–57
  infection in nonhuman primates,
    52–53
  reservoirs, 48–52, 54–56
  United States, 67
Egyptian fruit bats, *50*
electron microscopy, 30, 87
ELISA (enzyme-linked immunosorbent assay), 60, 61, 87
emerging pathogens, 87
encephalitis, 83, 87
endemic, 15, 87
enzyme-linked immunosorbent assay.
  See ELISA
epidemiologists, 20, 87
epidemiology, 8, 44–48
epithelium, 37, 87
Epomops franqueti, 54
euthanization, 28, 87
excreta, 80, 82, 87. *See also* guano

fatality rates, 87
  Crimean-Congo hemorrhagic
    fever, 76

dengue fever, 80
Ebola outbreaks, 18, 19, 65
Lassa fever, 82
yellow fever, 78
filoviridae, 87
filoviruses, *9*, 35–42
  allergic response, 11
  antibodies, 39
  bats as reservoir, 12, 49, 54–56
  clinical symptoms, 35–36
  detection of, 58–63
  modern plague, 8–11
  pathogenesis, 36–37
  phylogenetic tree, 45
  transmission, 40–42
  treatment for, 63–65
  viral proteins, 37–40
Flaviviridae, 76
fluorescein, 58, 88
"Four Corners Virus," 81
fruit bats, 54–56

Gabon, *14,* 21–22, 25, 47
Garrett, Laurie, 34
genes, 35, 88
genetic diversity, 44, 88
genomes, 35, 62–63, 88
Germany, 17
gorillas, 53, *55. See also* nonhuman
  primates
guano, 44, 54, 88

H5N1 (avian influenza), 6
hantavirus, 80–81
hantavirus hermorrhagic fever with
  renal syndrome (HFRS), 80
hemorrhage, 19, 88
hemorrhagic fevers, 88
  in Africa, 10
  biological warfare, 68–69
  Crimean-Congo hemorraghic fever
    virus, 75–76
  dengue, 78–80
  hantavirus, 80–81
  Lassa, 81–82

Rift Valley, 82–83
simian hemorrhagic fever, 28, 90
various, 75–84
yellow fever, 76–78
HEPA filters, 31, 70, 88
HFRS (hantavirus hermorrhagic fever
  with renal syndrome), 80
HFRS (renal syndrome), 80
histamines, 36, 88
The Hot Zone (Richard Preston), 34
humans, 56–57, 76
Hyalomma ticks, 75
Hypsignathus monstrosus, 54, 56

IFA. *See* indirect fluorescence assay
Ig. *See* immunoglobulins
immune response, 39, 88
immunoglobulins (Ig), 61–63, 88
incubation period, 35–36, 76, 88
index cases, 12, 17, 25, 26, 88
indirect fluorescence assay (IFA), 56,
  58–61, *59, 60,* 88
insect vectors, 46–47
interferon, 39, 88
international travel, 67–68
Ivory Coast, *14,* 20, 53

jaundice, 36, 41, 78, 83, 88

Karesh, William, 53
Kenya, 12, *14*
killed vaccine, 72, 88
Korean War, 80

laboratories
  biosafety level, 30–31
  Hazelton Research laboratory,
    28–30
  monkeys in. *See* monkeys
  nonhuman primates, 31, 33–34
Lassa, 17, 81–82
live attenuated vaccine, 72, 88

Mabalo, 17–18
macaques, 28, *29,* 73, 88. *See also* non-

human primates
Madagascar, 46
Marburg virus, 12–16, 44–45
  in Africa, *14*
  bat reservoir, 12, 49, 54, 56
  as biological weapon, 68–69
  emergence of, 12–16
  incubation period, 35–36, 67
  reservoir of, 48–52
  risk factors, 16
  subtypes of, 35
McCormick, Joe, 19, 20
Medecins sans Frontieres (Doctors without Borders), 13
media publicity, 34
Mexico, 76
monkeys
  detection experiments, 65. *See also*
    nonhuman primates
  Ebola Côte d'Ivoire, 53
  Ebola Reston, 46
  laboratory, 9, 28, 30, 31, 33–34
  Marburg virus, 12
  vaccine research, 73
  yellow fever, 76
morbidity, 68, 89
morphology, 8, 89
mortality rates, 89. *See also* fatality
  rates
  biological warfare, 68
  deadly diseases, 10–11, 66
  Ebola outbreaks, 23, 25, 26
  Marburg outbreak, 15
mosquitoes, 46, 76–79, *79*, 83
Mullis, Kary, 64
Myonycteris torquata, 54

Nabel, Gary, 73
National Institute of Allergy and
  Infectious Diseases, 74
naturally acquired infections, 89
necropsy, 21, 28, 52, 89
Netherlands, 15
nonhuman primates. *See also specific*
  primates

Ebola susceptibility, 72
evidence of infection, 52–53
filovirus reservoir, 48–49, 52–53
and human Ebola cases, 25
laboratory, 31, 33–34
North Korea, 69
nosocomial infections, 18, 23, 89

Outbreak (movie), 34

pandemics, 6
pathogenesis, 36–37, 70, 89
pathogens, 30–31, 66, 83–84
PCR (polymerase chain reaction), 89
peridomestic animals, 51, 89
phagocytes, 70, 89
Philippines, 26, 28, 33, 34, 46
phylogenetic tree, *45*, 46, 89
pigs, 26, 46
plants, 51
poaching, 53, 89
Poe, Edgar Allen, 40
polymerase(s), 64, 89
polymerase chain reaction (PCR),
  61–62, *63*, 64
Preston, Richard, 34
primates. *See* nonhuman primates
primatologists, 52, 53, 89
primers, 64, 89
Psammotettix species, 51
Pygmies, 56–57

"Red Death," 40–41
Reed, Walter, 78
Republic of Congo, 25
researchers, *71*
reservoirs, 89
  bats, 12, 49, 54–56
  of CCHF, 75–76
  Ebola virus, 48–52
  Marburg virus, 48–52
  nonhuman primate, 48–49, 52–53
  plants, 51–52
  rodents, 80–82
  yellow fever, 76

Reston, Virginia, 28, 66
Rift Valley fever, 82–83
ring vaccination, 73, 89
RNAses, 62, 90
RNA virus, 35, 47, 90
rodents, 80–82
Rousettus aegypticus, 50, 56
Russia, 75

Salmonella typhi, 8
SARS (severe acute respiratory syndrome), 6
Saudi Arabia, 82
savannah, 46, 90
secondary cases, 12, 90
secretion, 37, 90
sensitivity, 58, 62, 90
serological evidence, 16, 23, 46, 50–51, 90
seroprevalence, 46, 52, 56–57, 90
serum, 58, 61, 64, 90
severe acute respiratory syndrome (SARS), 6
SHF (simian hemorrhagic fever), 28, 90
shock, 8, 36, 90
simian hemorrhagic fever (SHF), 28, 90
South Africa, 12, *14*
South America, *77, 78*
Soviet Union, 13, 69
specificity, 58, 62, 90
strain, 44, 90
subclinical disease, 57, 90
substrate, 60, 61, 90
subtype, 35, 44–46, 48, 90
Sudan
   1976 Ebola outbreak, 18–20
   2004 Ebola outbreak, 25–26
   bat reservoir, 54
   Ebola outbreaks, 9–10, *14*
   Ebola Sudan, 49
   Marburg virus outbreak, *14*
Switzerland, 21

symptoms
   asymptomatic, 54, 86
   clinical, 35–36, 68

Tadarida (mops) trevori, 54
Taq polymerase, 64
T cell, 70, 90
template, 64, 91
terrorism, 68–69
tertiary case, 22, 91
tests, 58–61
thermophiles, 64, 91
ticks, 75
transfusions, 64, 91
transmission
   bats, 54–56
   biological warfare, 68
   Ebola virus, 42, 67–68
   filoviruses, 40–42
   insect vectors, 46–47
   Lassa virus, 82
   research, 70
transovarial transmission, 75, 91
treatment, 63–65

Uganda, *14,* 15, 23, *24,* 26, *27t*
United States
   biological warfare, 69
   dengue outbreak, 79
   Ebola outbreaks, 10, 20, 28–34
   hantavirus, 81
   hemorrhagic fever research, 83
   media publicity, 34
   vaccine development, 66–67
   yellow fever, 76–77
USAMRIID (U.S. Army Medical Research Institute of Infectious Diseases), 28, 33, 91

vaccines, 66–74, 91
   biological warfare, 68–69
   challenges, 69–72
   deadly diseases, 6–7
   production of, 73–74

reasons for development, 66–69
   types of, 72–73
vCJD (Creutzfeldt-Jakob disease), 6
vectors, 46–47, *50,* 91
viral envelope, 37, 91
viral proteins, 37–40
viremia, 41, 91
virulence, 20, 39, 91

West Nile Virus, 67
World Health Organization, 18

yellow fever

Africa, 17
arthropod vectors, 46
endemic areas, *77*
hemorrhagic fever, 76–78
mosquitoes, *79*
"Red Death," 41
Yemen, 82
Yucatán Peninsula, 76

Zaire, 9, 17
Zimbabwe, 12, *14*
zoonosis, 82, 91

About the Author

Tara C. Smith obtained her B.S in Biology in 1998 from Yale University, where she carried out research on the molecular epidemiology of *Streptococcus pyogenes*. In 2002, she earned her Ph.D. at the Medical College of Ohio under the tutelage of Dr. Michael Boyle and Dr. Darren Sledjeski. Her doctoral studies focused on group A streptococci, specifically virulence factor regulation in response to biological selection pressures. Dr. Smith carried out post-doctoral research at the University of Michigan with Dr. Betsy Foxman and Dr. Carl Marrs, studying the molecular epidemiology of the group B streptococcus, *Streptococcus agalactiae*. She has published several papers in scientific journals as a result of her research. Currently, Dr. Smith is an Assistant Professor in the department of epidemiology at the University of Iowa, and a member of the Center for Emerging Infectious Diseases. Her current research investigates a group of hypervariable genes in *S. agalactiae*. Other interests include zoonotic diseases. In addition, Dr. Smith is married and the mother of two children. She lives with her family near Iowa City, Iowa.

About the Consulting Editor

Hilary Babcock, M.D., M.P.H., is an assistant professor of medicine at Washington University School of Medicine and the Medical Director of Occupational Health for Barnes-Jewish Hospital and St. Louis Children's Hospital. She received her undergraduate degree from Brown University and her M.D. from the University of Texas Southwestern Medical Center at Dallas. After completing her residency, chief residency, and Infectious Disease fellowship at Barnes-Jewish Hospital, she joined the faculty of the Infectious Disease division. She completed an M.P.H. in Public Health from St. Louis University School of Public Health in 2006. She has lectured, taught, and written extensively about infectious diseases, their treatment, and their prevention. She is a member of numerous medical associations and is board certified in infectious disease. She lives in St. Louis, Missouri.